Lothar-Rüdiger Lütge

A Conscious Choice for Faith

The Deliberate Return to God
as Salvation from Crisis

Publisher: BoD • Books on
Demand GmbH, In de Tarpen 42,
22848 Norderstedt
Printed by: Libri Plureos GmbH,
Friedensallee 273, 22763
Hamburg

ISBN: 978-3-7597-9494-9

"Let nothing disturb you,
Let nothing frighten you,
All things are passing away:
God never changes.
Patience obtains all things
Whoever has God lacks nothing;
God alone suffices."

St. Teresa of Avila (1515 - 1582, Spain)

Preface

In the midst of a world marked by the disintegration of traditional values and a growing sense of disorientation, Western civilization stands at a crossroads. "Choosing to Believe poses the provocative question: Can conscious belief in a personal God be the salvation from the current crisis?

This book shows how the loss of faith and the resulting nihilism are plunging our society into chaos. It offers clear, practical guidance and inspiring examples for those looking for a way out. Discover how faith can offer not only personal fulfillment and stability, but also a return to absolute values and normative orientation.

Be inspired by the stories of people who have rediscovered their faith and experienced profound changes in their lives. "A Deliberate Choice for Faith is not just a book, it is a wake-up call--for you, for your family, and for our society.

Table of Contents

5.5 Conclusion of the Chapter

Chapter 6:
Additional Topics
and Practical Guidance

6.1 Introduction
6.2 Continuing Spiritual Practices
6.3 Faith in the Modern World
6.4 Practical Lifestyle Guidelines
6.5 Community and Social
    Involvement
6.6 Conclusion of the Chapter

Chapter 7:
Conclusion and Outlook

7.1 Review of the Journey
7.2 Personal Reflection and Application
7.3 Outlook and Inspiration
7.4 Concluding Remarks

Appendix

The Story of Rosalind Wright Picard
The Conversion of Ayaan Hirsi Ali:
A Plea for Faith

The Central Message

The central message of this book is as follows:

God is the Creator and Lord of the world, and we can choose to acknowledge this and thereby save ourselves, our society, and our culture.

All subsequent sections of the book are designed to further explain and contextualize this central idea. To this end, a structured format has been chosen in which many different aspects of the topic are presented in a clear and concise manner, considered from different angles, and then elaborated upon. This leads to a deliberate repetition of content when dealing with individual topics and concepts, in order to present them in a kaleidoscopic manner and thus to treat and explain them as comprehensively and in as much depth as possible. It is assumed that the average reader has little religious knowledge and little religious experience. This is therefore not a convenient "reader" in the usual sense, but a systematic collection of arguments and material in support of the central message, which we can formulate in a slightly more sophisticated way as follows:

1. Faith in God as Creator and Sustainer of the world is the way out of our existential social crisis.

2. This faith is open to all of us, because each person can decide to believe in God at any time through a conscious act of will.

This book is therefore intended to clarify certain facts and thus provide a kind of decision-making aid, but it is not intended to be missionary! On the contrary, no one should be persuaded or encouraged to do anything. Everyone decides for himself and on his own responsibility. This is the only way to consciously and willingly believe in God. One must really want to believe! Voluntarily! Out of insight and conviction.

And because the book has no missionary claim, it has even less claim to propagate a particular faith. It is neutral with regard to religions and denominations. There is, however, one important requirement: that the God of whom we speak must be the transcendent Creator and Sustainer of the world, and that this God must be recognized and worshipped as a person, as an individual being with consciousness and will. For only this God fulfills the indispensable conditions that are absolutely necessary for the salvation of us human beings and for the salvation of our world. All other concepts of God explicitly do not fulfill these conditions, because they lack either the transcendent or the personal component. In concrete terms, this means that all pantheistic conceptions of God and all conceptions of an impersonal, anonymous divine power as a causal or immanent factor in creation are not sufficient to solve our acute crisis of meaning and existence. We need God as our counterpart! We need Him as the Lord of the world who has given us rules and guidelines for our lives. Only in this way can we escape the rapidly spreading nihilism that threatens to devour us all.

This non-negotiable requirement for the image of God automatically limits the number of possible religions. In particular, the three monotheistic religions remain: Judaism, Christianity, and Islam, because they all appeal to a personal God and see Him as the Creator and Sustainer of the world. And since this book is especially addressed to the most threatened and endangered people of the Western world, and since this culture was primarily built on the foundation of Christianity, it is only natural that in the further course of the book special reference is made to the God defined by Christianity. More specifically, there are many references to Roman Catholic Christianity simply because that is the faith with which the author is most personally familiar. No exclusive claims are made.

As a preface to his own remarks and as a vivid illustration of the current crisis in which Europe and the Western world find themselves, the content of a detailed interview given by the historian and publicist David Engels to the television station 'Hoch2TV' on July 26, 2024 is summarized. This is followed by a text in which David Engels' central statements on the opening of the 2024 Olympic Games in Paris are also condensed and summarized. His original article on this topic appeared in 'Tichys Einblick' on July 27, 2024. The texts are not quoted verbatim or reproduced in their original form; rather, the content is presented in an edited and condensed form in order to make the central ideas clear.

This book is the result of extensive and constructive communication. Therefore, in addition to the author, there are other unnamed contributors. For this reason, the plural is used at various points in the text when the author is mentioned.

No prior knowledge is required to read this book, but since it is not so much for amusing entertainment, but primarily for information and reflection on quite serious topics, a certain amount of patient attention is expected from the reader. After all, it's about everything! Either the individual and society will succeed in regaining a firm foundation by returning to the source of our being, God, and confronting the nothingness of nihilism with the truth of God, in which case salvation is in sight. Or it will not succeed, in which case God have mercy on us, for then all will be lost, both for the individual and for society and culture as a whole, which will sink into the dystopian chaos of non-being.

Foreword on the Current Situation

The Crisis of the West - An Overview of the Theses of Prof. Dr. David Engels

In recent decades we have witnessed a profound transformation of our society, characterized by the loss of traditional values and the dissolution of cultural identities. These developments have led to a crisis of meaning that affects both individuals and entire communities. Prof. Dr. David Engels, a renowned historian and cultural philosopher, has highlighted this problem in his works and analyses. His theses offer valuable insights and form an important basis for the argumentation of this book.
Prof. Dr. David Engels' analysis in ten points

Cultural cycle theory: Engels sees Western civilization as being in its late phase, comparable to the final phase of the Roman Republic. This phase is characterized by decadence, moral decay, and political instability, indicating an impending period of conflict. He warns that we are in a situation similar to that of ancient Rome and that a change in thinking is necessary to prevent a complete collapse.

Comparative historical analysis: The study of past civilizations reveals parallels to our present, including mass immigration, demographic decline, and the breakdown of traditional family structures. Engels emphasizes that these historical parallels can help us understand the current crisis and take appropriate measures to avoid similar mistakes.

Technocratic elites: Engels criticizes the technocratic elites in Europe as undemocratic and ideologically anti-Western. In his view, these elites pursue their own interests and promote a global agenda that undermines cultural and national identities. Engels calls for a return to democratic principles and greater popular participation in political decision-making.

Loss of Identity and Universalism: The EU is criticized as an attempt to create a universalist state that neglects Western identity. Engels argues that this universalism leads to the loss of cultural diversity and the uprooting of people. He advocates a "Western patriotism" that preserves Europe's cultural identity and traditional values.

Return to tradition: Engels argues for a conscious and rational return to traditional values and transcendence in order to halt the disintegration of civilization. He sees the revival of religious and cultural traditions as the key to stabilizing society and creating a new sense of community.

Erosion of traditions: According to Engels, the deliberate dismantling of traditions leads to cultural disorientation and nihilism. He describes how the destruction of traditional institutions such as family, religion, and community leads to a loss of meaning and direction. This is very much in line with our comments in the first chapter, where we described the disintegration of values and norms and the dissolution of family structures.

Role of the EU: While Engels supports European cooperation in principle, he criticizes its current implementation and the ideology behind it. He argues for a greater emphasis on defending Western values and interests, while warning of the dangers of excessive centralization.

Historical parallels: Engels sees recurring patterns in history in which civilizations pass through phases of transcendence and immanence. He expects a similar development for the West, in which the current phase of immanence can be overcome by a return to transcendence. This view supports our argument in chapter two, where we explained the need for a transcendent reference point.

The Ambivalence of Restoration: A return to traditional values is not the ideal solution, but a necessary response to disintegration. Engels recognizes the ambivalence of this restoration, but insists that it offers an alternative to the current cultural and moral decay.

Critique of Modern Populism: Engels recognizes the accuracy of many diagnoses of modern populism, but criticizes the unrealistic solutions proposed. He advocates realistic and feasible approaches to overcoming the current crisis and renewing society.

The opening of the 2024 Olympic Games - an example of the decline of civilization:

Prof. Dr. David Engels describes the opening of the 2024 Olympic Games in Paris as a symbol of Europe's cultural decline. The event was marked by blasphemous and grotesque performances that reflected the decadence and aesthetics of a Rome choking on its own perversity. The advertising for the Olympics, which showed Paris without its church domes and crosses, already pointed to a conscious removal of religious symbols. The security measures, which excluded millions of people from the city and sealed off entire neighborhoods to prevent attacks, reinforced the impression of an overbearing and controlling state.

The artistic design of the opening ceremony was full of distasteful and controversial elements. Arielle Dombasle's multi-million-dollar interpretation of Beethoven's "Ode to Joy" was the first major media flop, featuring embarrassing choreography and ridiculous gestures. In several places in France, train lines to Paris were disrupted by suspected left-wing "activists," causing major logistical problems. Another embarrassing mishap was the Olympic flag being hoisted upside down, which Engels symbolized as the general incompetence of the French government.

The actual opening ceremony was dominated by a postmodern aesthetic that Engels describes as a "debacle. A feminist gallery of ancestors, an erotically whispered Marseillaise, and floating piles of garbage were just some of the bizarre elements. The culmination of tastelessness was a blasphemous re-enactment of the Last Supper and the presentation of a plump, blue-tinted Dionysus. Engels sees this event as a symbol of the "fin de règne" and the cultural decay of the West, which is leading itself ad absurdum.

Conclusion: The theses and observations of Prof. Dr. David Engels underline the necessity of a return to traditional values and a conscious reorientation towards transcendent principles. They provide a sound basis for the argumentation of this book and clarify why a conscious act of faith in a personal God is a rational and necessary response to the current crisis. This is consistent with our discussion in chapter two, where we present faith as a conscious and rational choice that can lead us out of moral and cultural decline.

Introduction

In a world marked by chaos, meaninglessness, and disorientation, this book aims to offer you a way out. Perhaps you often feel lost in a society that has abandoned its traditional values and norms. Perhaps you feel the effects of a culture that no longer offers clear guidelines and where everything seems relative. This book seeks to offer you a new perspective-a way back to stability, meaning, and direction.

We live in a time when many of us feel that our culture and society are in crisis. Families are breaking up, communities are disintegrating, and many people feel isolated and without real connections. Selfishness and self-centeredness dominate social life, while civility, discipline, and mutual respect are in increasingly short supply. In this book we want to explore why this is so and how we can find a way out.

Our answer lies in belief in a personal God. This term may be new or strange to you. A personal God is a transcendent being who exists beyond space and time and who created the universe, the world, and humanity. This God is not just an abstract idea, but a conscious Creator who has given us rules to live by and to whom we must answer after our physical death.

Rational considerations regarding belief in God:

It is understandable that in our modern and post-modern world, belief in a personal God is often seen as naive or irrational. However, there are good reasons to show that such belief can be perfectly rational and meaningful. Many materialistic and biologistic-evolutionary models of explaining the world run into considerable mathematical difficulties. For example, the time since the Big Bang is not long enough to explain the complex evolution of life and consciousness by chance alone. The mathematical probability that our existence is the result of pure chance is extremely low. This does not prove anything in the strict sense, but it shows that the foundations of modern and postmodern thought are not sacrosanct and are often based on unproven assumptions.

Therefore, conscious belief in God is at least as rational as the nihilism to which many people in our society subscribe. This belief offers not only a deeper sense of meaning, but also a more stable foundation for moral and ethical values. When you choose to believe in God, you are making a well-

considered and well-founded decision that can enrich and give direction to your life.

The purpose of this book:

Western societies are in a state of profound dys-
function. The almost absolute and unconditional
liberalism that allows everything and makes everything possible for everyone has largely undermined
traditional customs and norms. The consequences
are widespread and profound. Families are breaking up, marriages are failing, and the social fabric is
unraveling. Stable communities are being replaced
by loose, temporary ties that create no real bonds
or responsibilities.

This disintegration extends to countries and states.
Ethnic and cultural identities are diluted in dysfunc-
tional multicultural structures formed by people
from different cultural backgrounds. This leads to a
general loss of a sense of belonging and community, and isolation increases.

This cultural disintegration is accompanied by a
dramatic decline in education and culture, in style
and manners, in honor and appropriate behavior. A
general coarsening is spreading. Clothing, appear-
ance, behavior and manners have reached a

frighteningly low level. Civility, order, style, discipline, and propriety have become foreign words, hardly understood or appreciated in our society. The meaning and purpose of life have disappeared from the consciousness of many people, replaced by the pursuit of immediate gratification. There are no objective values anymore, everything is relative. Public life is increasingly disintegrating, and no one feels responsible for anything. This irresponsibility also prevails in business and the economy. At the same time, we are experiencing an increasingly intrusive state, whose representatives behave like absolute rulers and no longer tolerate any criticism.

In the midst of this cultural and moral decline, it is clear that the solution cannot be found within the existing system. Such a solution must come from outside, from a transcendent source that can give us orientation and stability again. The conscious decision to believe in a personal God who gives us transcendent values and norms is the key to overcoming this crisis. This belief is not a blind act, but a rational decision based on the realization that without this transcendent foundation we will slide into nihilism and meaninglessness.

Traditional religions, especially Christianity, offer us this knowledge and guidance. They contain valuable teachings and principles that can help us put our lives and our societies back on a stable and meaningful footing. This book shows how we can consciously re-integrate these transcendent values into our lives. It offers practical guidance on how individuals, families, and communities can live this faith and thereby achieve a new order and meaning.

Let us walk this path together and discover how consciously choosing to believe can transform our lives and heal our society.

Chapter 1:
The Crisis of Modernity

1.1 Introduction to the Crisis

Our modern society is experiencing a profound crisis that manifests itself on many levels. The traditional values and norms that once formed the foundation of our culture and communities are disintegrating. This crisis is not the result of a single problem, but rather the result of a complex interaction of many factors that together present an unprecedented challenge.

The disintegration of traditional values and norms

In the past, values and norms such as honor, respect, discipline, and responsibility were central to social life. These values provided guidance and helped foster a sense of community and cohesion. Today, however, we see that these traditional values are eroding. Relativism and a culture of arbitrariness have taken hold. Clear standards for guiding individual and collective behavior have largely disappeared. The concept of morality seems antiquated, and the pursuit of instant gratification and personal freedom without regard for others has grown in importance.

Disintegration of Families and Communities

A particularly alarming aspect of this crisis is the breakdown of families and communities. Family structures, once considered the cornerstone of society, are crumbling. Divorce rates are high, and more and more children are growing up in broken or single-parent households. The traditional role of the family as a place of stability and transmission of values is increasingly challenged. At the same time, we are witnessing the erosion of communities. Places where people support each other and come together are declining. Loneliness is on the rise, and many people feel isolated and without real connections.

The Dominance of Selfishness and Self-Centeredness

These social changes are accompanied by an increasing dominance of selfishness and self-centeredness. In a culture that values individualism and personal freedom above all else, altruistic values and the common good are often neglected. People are more concerned with satisfying their own needs and desires than with taking responsibility for their fellow human beings. This leads to a fragmentation of society and a lack of social cohesion.

Decline in Aesthetics, Decency, Dignity and Style

The social decline is also evident in the erosion of aesthetics, decency, dignity and style in all facets of life. Everything is becoming vulgar and tasteless. Clothing, art, architecture, and entertainment are increasingly characterized by arbitrariness and superficiality. Society is neglected and loses its sense of beauty and elegance. Decency and courtesy have become rare, and respectful interaction is replaced by rude and selfish behavior. The dignity of the individual is often disregarded and there is a general lack of respect for others.

General arbitrariness and levelling of values

There is a pervasive sense of arbitrariness, where everything seems equal and nothing seems to have consequences. People live as if there are no higher goals or purposes. There are no clear guidelines to provide orientation. Identities dissolve, and a uniform mass of opinions and cultures emerges, in which individual and cultural differences are blurred. The loss of a sense of home and belonging leads to increasing alienation and isolation.

Loss of Higher Purpose, Meaning, and Goal

The overarching purpose, meaning, and direction in life have completely disappeared. Many people no longer have a clear idea of why they are living and what they should be working toward. The pursuit of personal satisfaction has replaced the search for deeper meaning. There are no longer any objective values; everything is relative and depends on individual preferences and opinions. Public life is increasingly disintegrating, and no one feels responsible for anything. This irresponsibility also prevails in business and the economy. At the same time, we are experiencing an increasingly intrusive state, whose representatives behave like absolute rulers and no longer tolerate any criticism.

This deep crisis shows that the solution cannot be found within the existing system. Such a solution must come from outside, from a transcendent source that can give us orientation and stability again.

1.2 Causes of the Crisis

The current crisis in our society has deep-rooted causes that manifest themselves in two main currents: liberal individualism and relativism. These

two schools of thought have contributed significantly to the erosion of the traditional values and
norms that once formed the foundation of our culture.

Liberal Individualism

Liberal individualism is a way of thinking that places
personal freedom and individual self-actualization
above all else. In its extreme form, it promotes the
credo that anyone can do whatever they want as
long as they do not directly restrict the freedom of
another. This idea has had a significant impact on
social mores and norms in recent decades.

In a society that values individual freedom above all
else, traditional values such as discipline, responsibility, and consideration for others are increasingly
seen as restrictive. The emphasis on personal well-
being and satisfaction leads to a fragmentation of
society. Each person pursues his or her own goals
without regard for the needs and well-being of the
community.

This development has a significant impact on social
mores and norms. Rules and behaviors that were
once taken for granted are now seen as restrictions
on personal freedom. The result is a society in

which anything goes and moral reference points have been lost. Decency, courtesy, and mutual respect are often seen as outdated concepts that stand in the way of personal development.

In practice, this leads to a culture that prioritizes instant gratification and personal freedom over consideration for others. The collective good is often neglected, and the social bonds that hold communities together are weakened. Liberal individualism promotes an attitude in which the individual is central, leading to increasing isolation and alienation.

Relativism

Relativism is another major cause of the current crisis. This philosophical movement denies the existence of objective, universal values and norms. Instead, it claims that all values and norms are relative and depend on individual or cultural preferences.

The loss of objective values has far-reaching consequences for society. When everything is relative and there are no universal standards, society loses its moral orientation. There are no longer universal rules to guide people's behavior. Everyone decides for themselves what is right and wrong, leading to moral chaos.

Relativism promotes a culture of arbitrariness in which everything is equal and nothing is considered better or worse. This leads to a flattening of all values, where no idea or belief is considered superior. In such a society, it is difficult to find common goals and values that unite people and give them direction.

The idea that everything is relative also undermines trust in traditional institutions and authorities. When there are no objective truths, religion, science, and other systems of knowledge lose their authority. This leads to a general skepticism and distrust of established structures, which further undermines social stability.

In a system characterized by liberalism and relativism, we are left with only relative values. However, these values are not enough to free us from the deep crisis we are in. We cannot pull ourselves out of the swamp by our own hair, like Baron Munchausen. To find a firm foothold, we need a fixed point outside our ailing system. That anchor lies in transcendence, in God. Only a transcendent, personal God can give us the orientation and stability we need to overcome the current crisis.

1.3 Effects of the Crisis

The deep crisis in our society has multiple and far-reaching effects on the individual, the community, and the entire culture. These effects are evident in people's daily experiences and have a fundamental impact on human coexistence and personal development.

On the individual

Isolation and disconnection: In modern society, many people feel increasingly isolated and disconnected. Traditional social structures that once provided community and support are disintegrating. Families, which once served as central places of cohesion and security, are often broken or no longer exist in their traditional form. The result is widespread loneliness. Many people live alone, without regular contact with family or friends. Virtual communication through social media often cannot compensate for this isolation and instead leads to superficial relationships that do not offer deep emotional connections.

Loss of meaning and purpose: The loss of traditional values and increasing relativism have left many people without a clear sense of purpose in their lives. Without firm moral and ethical reference points, many feel lost and disillusioned. The pursuit of instant gratification and material success has pushed spiritual and existential questions into the background. People search for meaning and fulfillment, but often find only temporary satisfaction in consumerism and superficial pleasures. The inner drive to achieve something greater and more meaningful is waning, and many people are experiencing a profound crisis of meaning.

On the society

Disintegration of communities: The breakdown of traditional social structures has far-reaching implications for society as a whole. Communities that were once held together by shared values and goals are disintegrating. Social cohesion declines and a sense of belonging is lost. Stable communities are replaced by loose, temporary ties that do not create real bonds or responsibilities. The result is a fragmented society in which individual interests take precedence over the common good. Social cohesion, which is necessary to overcome common challenges and maintain a functioning community, is increasingly weakened.

Crises of ethnic and cultural identity: In an increasingly globalized and multicultural world, many people are experiencing a crisis of ethnic and cultural identity. The traditional cultural roots that once provided a sense of identity and belonging are often diluted or lost. The result is an identity crisis in which people find it difficult to find their place in society. Cultural diversity, originally seen as an enrichment, is often perceived as a threat, and conflicts arise between different ethnic and cultural groups. The search for identity and belonging becomes a challenge in a world that is constantly changing and in which traditional points of reference are disappearing.

On education and culture

The decline of education, style and customs: The crisis is also having a profound impact on education and cultural standards. Education, once seen as a path to personal and social advancement, is losing its meaning. Educational standards are falling and basic knowledge and skills are being lost. This is evident not only in formal educational institutions, but also in general cultural life. Style, manners and good etiquette, once considered a sign of education and cultural heritage, are being neglected. They are replaced by vulgar language, disrespect, and a general lack of courtesy.

General brutalization and decline in standards of behavior and manners: The brutalization of society manifests itself in a general decline in standards of behavior and manners. Public debates and personal interactions are increasingly characterized by aggression, disrespect, and intolerance. The ability to treat each other in a civilized and respectful manner is being lost. This is evident in all areas of public and private life - from political discourse and social media to everyday interactions in public spaces. The decline in standards of behavior and manners contributes to the general deterioration of the social climate and makes it more difficult to build a harmonious society based on solidarity.

The effects of this crisis are pervasive, affecting every aspect of human life. Without a fundamental change in the values and norms that shape our society, this crisis will continue to deepen and further undermine our ability to function as a community.

1.4 Examples and Illustrations

To make the impact of the current crisis in our society more tangible, it is important to look at concrete examples from everyday life and supporting statistics and studies. These illustrate the depth of the changes and problems.

Concrete examples from today's society

Examples of the breakdown of family structures:

A clear example of the breakdown of traditional family structures is the high divorce rate. In many Western countries, almost every second marriage ends in divorce. This has far-reaching consequences for the families involved, especially for the children. Studies show that children from broken families are more likely to suffer from emotional and psychological problems, do worse in school, and have more difficulty forming stable relationships. Single parents often face enormous challenges, both financially and emotionally, which further affects family stability.

Another example is the increasing number of children growing up in patchwork families or with changing partners. The stability and continuity once taken for granted is no longer a given for many children. This leads to a sense of insecurity and disorientation as there are no fixed points of reference.

Illustrations of the general brutalization and loss of politeness and discipline:

The erosion of civility and discipline is evident in public spaces. Public transportation, shopping malls and streets are the scene of aggressive behavior and lack of respect. People cut in line, hurl insults, and show little regard for others. These behaviors are also reflected in road traffic, where recklessness and aggression are increasingly the norm.

Another example is social media communication. Platforms such as Facebook, X and Instagram are often characterized by hateful and offensive comments. The anonymity of the Internet encourages behaviors that are typically suppressed in face-to-face encounters. People feel emboldened to express more extreme opinions and verbally attack others without considering the consequences of their actions.

Loss of style and taste

A striking aspect of cultural decline is the loss of style and taste in clothing and general behavior. Clothing that was once reserved for specific occasions or activities is now worn out of context. One example is jeans, originally a garment for hard physical labor, which are now worn by people of all ages and in almost every situation. This uniformity reflects an indifference to situationally appropriate behavior.

Also noteworthy is the declining importance of gender-specific clothing. Women now rarely wear skirts and dresses, but mostly trousers, which were once reserved for men. At the same time, adult men are dressing like teenagers, resorting to bright colors and cultivating a very unmanly, androgynous style. This is not only a sign of changing fashion, but also of the dissolution of traditional gender roles.

Loss of education and general intellectual level:

Another alarming sign of the crisis is the decline in education and general intellectual standards. In many countries, educational attainment is declining and basic knowledge and skills are being lost. This is reflected not only in academic performance, but also in the quality of public debate and cultural life. The ability to understand and debate complex issues is declining.

Decline in public order and increase in everyday violence:

Public order is deteriorating and everyday violence is increasing dramatically. Knife attacks and murders have become commonplace, creating a sense of insecurity and fear among the population. The authority of state institutions is being undermined, while at the same time the authorities are brutally enforcing arbitrary rules. This paradoxical situation leads to a deep distrust of the institutions that are supposed to guarantee protection and security.

Excessive bureaucracy despite digitization:

Despite increasing digitization, bureaucracy is not being reduced, but rather processes and procedures are being increasingly delayed. Bureaucratic hurdles are increasing in both the public and private sectors, leading to inefficient processes and general frustration among citizens.

Statistics and studies
We can refer to various statistics and studies to support the above points:

Divorce rates: According to the German Federal Statistical Office, the divorce rate in Germany is around 40%, which means that almost every second marriage ends in divorce. Similar figures are found in many other Western countries.

Children's mental health: A study by the Robert Koch Institute shows that children from divorced families have an increased risk of mental illness and behavioral problems.

Behavioral studies in public spaces: Studies by the Max Planck Institute for Human Development have shown an increase in disrespectful behavior and aggression in public spaces.

Online behavior: A study by the University of Hohenheim found that about 30% of comments on social media can be classified as hateful or offensive. This trend towards the coarsening of online communication reflects a general deterioration in social interaction.

Education levels: OECD reports show that education levels are declining in many Western countries, which is reflected in lower performance in international comparative tests such as PISA.

Violence statistics: Police statistics show an increase in knife attacks and other acts of violence in public spaces, highlighting growing insecurity and the erosion of public order.

Bureaucracy and efficiency: Studies on the efficiency of public administration and business show that despite digitalization, bureaucracy is not decreasing, but often increasing, leading to inefficient processes and delays.

These examples and statistics illustrate the profound impact of the current crisis and show how widespread and deep-rooted these problems are. They illustrate the need for a fundamental change in our values and norms to reverse the negative trends and create a more stable, respectful society.

1.5 Conclusion of the Chapter

Summary of the Crisis:

In this chapter we have examined the profound crisis of our modern society, characterized by the breakdown of traditional values and norms, the disintegration of family structures and communities, and the dominance of selfishness and self-centeredness. These developments lead to isolation and lack of connection at the individual level, while society as a whole suffers from the disintegration of communities and ethnic and cultural identity crises. At the same time, we are experiencing a dramatic decline in education, style and morality, as well as a general coarsening and deterioration of standards of behavior and manners.

Concrete examples from everyday life and supporting statistics have illustrated the effects of this crisis: the high divorce rate, aggressive behavior in public spaces, the loss of style and taste, the decline in intellectual standards, the increase in everyday violence, and the overabundance of bureaucracy despite the advancing digitalization.

This deep crisis shows that in a system characterized by liberalism and relativism, there are only relative values. However, these values are not enough to free us from the deep crisis in which we find ourselves. We cannot pull ourselves out of the mire by our own bootstraps like Munchausen. In order to find a firm foothold, we need a fixed point outside of our ailing system. That anchor lies in transcendence, in God. Only a transcendent, personal God can provide the orientation and stability we need to overcome the current crisis.

Transition to the necessity of a way out.

In the face of this extensive and profound crisis, it is clear that a fundamental change is needed. We need a return to solid, transcendent values and norms that can give us guidance and support. In the next chapter we will look at how conscious faith in a personal God can make this change possible. We will explore how this faith can provide a sound and meaningful response to the current crisis, not only spiritually but also rationally.

Chapter 2:
The Possibility of a Way Out

2.1 Introduction to the Way Out

A brief summary of the crisis:

In the first chapter we examined the profound crisis of our modern society. This crisis is characterized by the breakdown of traditional values and norms, the disintegration of family structures and communities, and the dominance of selfishness and self-centeredness. We have shown the effects of these developments on the individual, society, and culture, and we have noted that in a system characterized by liberalism and relativism, only relative values are available. However, these values are not sufficient to free us from the deep crisis in which we find ourselves.

The need for a transcendent reference point:

In order to find a way out of the current crisis, a transcendental fixed point is needed - an orientation outside the existing system. A clear example of this is a ship in the middle of the sea, unable to see the shore. To navigate and orient itself, the crew needs a landmark outside the ship, such as a landmark on land or the fixed stars in the sky. These external landmarks make it possible to determine one's position and set a course. Without such landmarks, the ship drifts aimlessly and can easily get lost. Similarly, sailors have used the North Star to chart their course for centuries. The North Star is a fixed point in the sky that always points north, regardless of the ship's position. Without such a fixed point, reliable navigation would be impossible.

Other illustrative examples:

Another example is the concept of the compass. In the wilderness, with no recognizable landmarks, the compass provides a fixed reference point, magnetic north. This allows hikers and adventurers to determine their direction and find their way. Without the compass, they would risk getting lost and wandering aimlessly.

In science, too, there are fixed reference points that are essential to understanding the world. For example, the speed of light is a constant that serves as the unchanging basis for many physical equations. Without such constants, it would be impossible to make the precise and reliable calculations that form the basis of our scientific understanding.

A fixed point in the transcendent:

For our society, this means that we need a fixed point in the transcendent, with God. The universe, our world, and everything in it are part of a relative reality limited by space and time. Matter and energy, thoughts and ideas - all these are relative and have no absolute, objective values. This relativity is the source of our current crisis because it offers no fixed, unchanging points of reference.

Only that which exists outside this relative world can offer us an absolute fixed point. This transcendent being is God, the ultimate Creator of the relative world. God is the source and cause of relative existence and exists beyond space and time. This makes God the only fixed point that is unchanging and absolutely valid.

All other supposed fixed points are part of the relative world and therefore subject to erosion and interpretation. They cannot provide us with lasting guidance because they are themselves part of the problem they seek to solve. Relativistic values and systems have led us into the present misery, and only a transcendent, personal God can offer us the stability and orientation necessary to find our way out of this crisis.

This transcendent fixed point in God makes it possible to establish objective and unchanging values and norms that can serve as moral guidelines and guide people's behavior and decisions. Without this fixed point, there is a lack of clear and coherent orientation, which leads to moral and social chaos. Therefore, it is essential that we rely on God as our ultimate reference point in order to find guidance and stability and to overcome the present crisis.

2.2 The Conscious Act of Will

Faith as a rational choice:

Belief in a personal God is often seen as a purely emotional or traditional act. However, there are good reasons to understand faith as a conscious, rational choice. Faith for emotional reasons can be a romanticized notion that is not always sustainable. Conscious faith, on the other hand, is usually based on rational considerations.

In many cases, faith is adopted as part of a life tradition into which one is born. This often happens unconsciously, without ever being questioned. Those who believe for traditional reasons usually do not need our book because they already have faith. Our readers, on the other hand, probably do not believe in God and therefore need to make a conscious decision to believe. Because faith will not come to them by itself, out of nowhere. God does not come to people; people have to go to God.

In the Bible, Jesus Christ says: "Ask, and it will be given to you; seek, and you will find; knock, and the door will be opened to you. (Matthew 7:7-11). Faith in God is therefore a conscious act, a decision, a path that a person must take. The conscious decision to believe is a completely natural process. Once a person realizes that without God he has gotten himself into a difficult, untenable, hopeless situation from which there is no way out on his own, he can turn to God and say: "Sorry, I made a mistake in denying you and excluding you from my life. I see that I overestimated myself. I am not the autonomous being I thought I was. I want to return to you, God, and ask you to help me in my life, ask you to show me the way with your commandments". This approach is driven primarily by reason and only secondarily by emotion.

An appropriate parable for this is the parable of the prodigal son, told by Jesus Christ himself. A young man leaves his home, squanders his inheritance, and falls into poverty and despair. Recognizing his mistake, he returns in repentance to his father, who welcomes him with open arms. This is a powerful image of the conscious decision to believe in God. The prodigal son represents the person who has turned away from God but finds his way back through conscious reflection and recognition.

What is faith?

Faith is believing something to be true. In this sense, we always believe when we believe something to be true. Belief is a completely natural and everyday process that is an integral part of our lives. The often-cited contrast between belief and knowledge distorts reality because we actually know very few things. If we define knowledge as personal opinion and certainty, we realize that many of our beliefs are based on faith. For example, very few of us "know" as a personal belief that the earth revolves around the sun. We believe it because cosmologists have explained it to us. And it is the same with many other things in our daily lives.

So believing is something quite normal, and we do it all the time. Even believing that there is no God is a belief because no one has ever proven it. Just because such an idea is popular today doesn't mean it's right.

In summary, conscious belief in God means that one rationally chooses this belief because one has recognized the relativity and inadequacy of worldly values and systems. One recognizes the need for a transcendent fixed point and consciously chooses the path of faith in order to find orientation, support, and a deeper meaning in life.

Philosophical Justifications:

Belief in God is not merely an emotional or traditional phenomenon, but can have a solid philosophical and scientific basis. Several arguments from philosophy and science support the idea of a personal God.

Cosmological argument: This argument states that everything that exists must have a cause. The universe exists, so it must have a cause external to the universe itself. This first cause, which is not itself caused, is called God. God is therefore the unmoved mover, the first cause that brought the universe into existence. This argument is based on the idea that there is a logical necessity for a first cause that is not itself caused and that stands outside the chain of causes and effects that we observe in the world.

Teleological argument: Also known as the design argument, this argument states that the universe and life exhibit such complexity and order that they could not have arisen by random processes. Instead, this order points to an intelligent designer who created the universe with a specific purpose and goal. The fine-tuning of natural laws, the complexity of biological systems, and the harmonious structure of the universe are interpreted as evidence for the existence of a designer. This argument emphasizes that the probability of such complex and purposeful structures arising by chance is extremely low.

Moral argument: This argument is based on the existence of objective moral values and duties. If there are objective moral values that exist independently of human opinions, then there must be a source of these values that is not itself part of the natural world. This source is said to be God. God is the moral lawgiver who establishes objective moral values and gives people moral guidance. Without God, moral values would be relative and subjective, leading to moral arbitrariness.

Ontological argument: This argument goes back to Anselm of Canterbury and is based on the idea that God must exist as the greatest conceivable being. If we can imagine God as the greatest and most perfect being, then that being must exist in reality, since an existing being is greater than a being that only exists in the imagination. Although this argument is often criticized as difficult to grasp, it has inspired many thinkers over the centuries and remains a significant contribution to the philosophy of religion.

Scientific Considerations:

Dr. Stephen Meyer and other scientists have made arguments that support belief in an intelligent designer on a scientific basis. These considerations show that belief in God is not inconsistent with scientific evidence, but can be supported by it.

Information Complexity in DNA: The discovery of information complexity in DNA is a strong argument for an intelligent designer. DNA contains complex and specific information that serves as the blueprint for living organisms. This complexity cannot be explained by random processes or self-organization, but points to an intelligent designer.

The fine-tuning of the universe: The fine-tuning of the fundamental constants in the universe points to intelligent design. The precision with which these constants are adjusted makes the existence of life possible. The probability that this fine-tuning occurred by chance is extremely low. Alternative explanations, such as the multiverse hypothesis, are speculative and do not offer a definitive solution.

Cosmological arguments: The origin of the universe, as demonstrated by the big bang theory and general relativity, points to a transcendent, personal God who is the cause of space, time, matter, and energy. These theories support the idea that the universe has a beginning and therefore requires a cause outside of itself.

Criticism of Neo-Darwinism: There are significant scientific doubts about neo-Darwinism, especially with regard to explaining major evolutionary changes. These doubts pave the way for alternative explanations, such as intelligent design. Scientists like Meyer argue that the complexity of life cannot be explained by random mutation and natural selection alone.

The role of information in biology: Information is a fundamental component of biology, comparable to matter and energy. This information suggests an intelligent origin, since our experience shows that information always originates from a mind. The existence of complex information in biological systems supports the assumption of an intelligent designer.

Problems of Origin Research: Research into the origin of life faces major challenges, especially in explaining the origin of the necessary information. Meyer argues that only an intelligent designer can account for this information complexity.

Refuting the Multiverse Hypothesis: The multiverse hypothesis is criticized because it does not provide an ultimate explanation for the fine-tuning of the universe and is based on many unproven theoretical postulates. This hypothesis only postpones the problem, not solves it.

These scientific considerations show that belief in God is not irrational, but is based on logical and sound arguments. Both philosophical and scientific considerations provide strong support for belief in a personal God.

Pragmatic Reasons:

Belief in a personal God can not only be justified philosophically and scientifically, but also offers practical benefits that can lead to a more fulfilling and meaningful life. There are several pragmatic reasons that support conscious belief in God as a rational choice.

Meaning and purpose in life: One of the greatest benefits of believing in God is the opportunity to find a deeper meaning and purpose in life. Belief in a Creator and a Higher Power who purposefully created the universe and life gives one's existence a deeper meaning beyond mere survival and the satisfaction of basic needs. People who believe in God often feel that they are part of a larger plan, which gives them direction and motivation.

Moral Orientation: Belief in God provides a clear moral orientation that is often lacking in modern society. Divine commandments and ethical guidelines provide firm and unchanging standards that guide behavior and help make moral decisions. This can contribute to a more just and harmonious co-existence and promote individual and collective well-being.

Community and belonging: Religious belief creates community and belonging. People who believe in God are often part of religious communities that provide support, friendship and a sense of belonging. These communities provide not only spiritual support, but also social and emotional support, which is particularly valuable in difficult times.

Psychological well-being: Studies have shown that religious belief and spiritual practices such as prayer and meditation can promote psychological well-being. People of faith often report a greater sense of purpose in life, greater satisfaction, and better stress management. Belief in God can provide comfort and hope during difficult times in life and build resilience in the face of crisis.

Ethics and social responsibility: Belief in God encourages ethical behavior and social responsibility. People of faith often feel an obligation to help others and make a positive contribution to society. This can lead to greater social cohesion and a more supportive community.

Long-term perspective: Belief in an afterlife and divine justice provides a long-term perspective beyond earthly life. This perspective can help put current challenges and suffering into perspective and look to the future with hope and confidence. It also provides a basis for moral action that transcends short-term personal gain.

In sum, belief in God offers many pragmatic benefits that can enrich individual lives and contribute to a better society. These benefits make belief in God a rational and rewarding choice that can promote both personal well-being and the collective good.

2.3 Transcendent Values and Standards

Definition and Meaning:

By transcendent values and norms we mean those principles that exist independently of human opinions and cultural differences. These values and norms are not of this world, but come from a higher, divine order. They are absolute, immutable, and universally valid. Examples of transcendent values and standards are

- Love: In the Christian sense, selfless, unconditional love for God and fellow human beings, as required by the commandment to love one's neighbor: "Love your neighbor as yourself" (Mark 12:31).

- Justice: A universal value that refers to the fair treatment of all people, regardless of their background. Justice means that everyone receives what is due and that injustice is actively combated.

- Truth: The search for and adherence to the truth, regardless of the consequences. Truth is a fundamental value considered divinely inspired in many religions and philosophies.

- Compassion: Compassion and active assistance to those in need. Mercy is considered a central value in Christianity and is closely related to love for one's fellow man.

- Sanctity of Life: The recognition and protection of life as a divine gift. This includes respect for life in all its forms, from conception to natural death.

- Humility: The recognition of one's limitations and devotion to God. Humility means correctly assessing one's place in the world and not elevating oneself above others.

These and other transcendent values and norms contrast with relativistic values, which can vary according to cultural context and individual opinion. In a world that is often characterized by subjective and changing values, transcendent values and norms provide a firm foundation and orientation.

Transcendent values and norms are therefore principles that transcend our worldly, cultural, and individual conceptions. They come from a higher, divine source and have universal and eternal validity. These values and norms are independent of people's changing opinions and fashions, and therefore provide an unchanging basis for moral and ethical behavior. In an age when many values and norms have become relative and fleeting, transcendent values provide a firm foundation on which to build our lives.

Transcendent values not only give stability to our lives, but also a deeper meaning. They show us that our actions and choices have a greater purpose that transcends our individual existence. By aligning ourselves with these higher principles, we can live meaningful and purposeful lives.

Absoluteness and immutability:

A key advantage of transcendent values is that they are absolute and unchanging. Unlike human values, which are often changeable, transcendental values always remain the same. They are not subject to the changing tides of time or cultural preferences. This gives them a constancy that is invaluable in the modern, ever-changing world.

While perceptions of justice, morality, and ethics may change according to culture and time, transcendent values remain constant. For example, values such as love of God and love of neighbor remain unchanged in their essence, regardless of external circumstances. These values are deeply rooted in the divine nature and divine will, and provide us with reliable guidance regardless of the social changes around us.

Transcendent values and norms stand in stark contrast to the ideas of liberalism, rationalism, and relativism that dominate modernity and postmodernity. While these philosophies are based on relative values and individual preferences, transcendent values provide a stable foundation that can free us from the destructive clutches of nihilism. By focusing on transcendent values, we transcend the relativity of the modern world and find a firm foothold that provides orientation and stability.

Moral Orientation:

Transcendent values serve as moral guidelines that shape our behavior and choices. They provide clear and unchanging standards that help us distinguish right from wrong. In a world of moral arbitrariness and relativism, these values give us clear direction and help us make moral decisions based on firm principles.

A central example is the commandment to love one's neighbor, which plays a key role in Christianity. This commandment calls us to love our fellow human beings and to treat them with respect and compassion. It provides a fixed standard for our behavior, regardless of personal preferences or social norms. Importantly, however, these transcendent values must always be considered within the broader God-given context. Charity, as described by Jesus Christ in the parable of the Good Samaritan, must be understood in its original context. The Good Samaritan cared for his neighbor at his doorstep, in his immediate environment, not for some needy person anywhere in the world. An overly broad interpretation could lead to excessive demands and damage to one's own resources and community.

Transcendent values and norms form a complex set of rules that must be considered and followed as a whole. It is counterproductive to separate out individual aspects and consider them in isolation. This often happens in liberalism, rationalism, and relativism, which themselves have no absolute values. In such cases, transcendent values are often taken out of context and misunderstood. In order to properly understand and apply transcendent values, it is necessary to turn to them fully and study them comprehensively in their respective religious contexts.

By being guided by transcendent values, we can live a life of moral integrity and meaning. These values not only provide us with moral guidance, but also help us to take responsibility for our actions and to act ethically, even when this means personal sacrifice or inconvenience. In a world of uncertainty and change, transcendent values provide the stability and guidance needed to live a fulfilling and meaningful life.

2.4 Belief in a Personal God

Characteristics of a Personal God:

Belief in a personal God is fundamentally different from abstract or pantheistic notions of a higher power. A personal God has specific characteristics that form the basis for a personal relationship between God and man. The essential characteristics of a personal God include

Personhood: Unlike an impersonal force, a personal God is a being with consciousness, will, intellect, and emotions. This personhood enables humans to have a personal relationship with God, to pray to Him, and to communicate with Him.

Creator and Sustainer: God is the Creator of the universe and all beings within it. He is also the sustainer of creation, continually sustaining it and giving it existence. This characteristic emphasizes the dependence of creation on God and his constant care.

Transcendence and Immanence: A personal God is both transcendent, existing outside and independent of the material world, and immanent, being present and active in the world. This dual quality enables God to direct the universe while at the same time intervening in and relating to the lives of human beings.

Omnipotence: A personal God is omnipotent, meaning that He has unlimited power. This omnipotence enables God to create and direct the universe. It gives us the assurance that nothing is beyond God's control and that he is able to do anything according to his will.

Omniscience: God is omniscient, which means that He knows everything-past, present, and future. This characteristic implies that God knows the thoughts, feelings, and actions of all people. His omniscience enables him to make wise and just decisions that transcend our limited human understanding.

Moral goodness: A personal God is imbued with moral goodness. This goodness is manifested in his love, justice, mercy, and care for his creation. God's moral goodness provides us with a perfect example and standard for our own moral conduct.

Why Other Images of God Are Not Enough:

While belief in a personal God provides a clear and stable foundation for moral and ethical guidance, other images of God cannot do so in the same way. Here are some reasons why pantheistic, abstract, or impersonal concepts of God do not provide the desired escape from the relativism and nihilism of modernity and postmodernity:

Pantheism: Pantheism sees God as identical with the universe or nature. In this view, God is not transcendent, but a completely immanent energy or power. This idea cannot provide clear moral guidelines because it does not allow for a personal relationship between God and man. Without a personal God, there is no moral authority to establish objective and absolute values.

Impersonal force: Concepts of God as an impersonal force or energy lack the qualities of consciousness, volition, and moral goodness. An impersonal force cannot make moral decisions or set ethical standards. It does not provide the basis for a personal relationship through which humans can experience moral direction and meaning.
God as Soul Energy: The idea of God as soul energy or universal consciousness often remains vague and abstract. Such concepts can be inspiring, but they do not provide concrete moral guidelines or a firm basis for ethical behavior. In practice, they tend to be interpreted relativistically, leading to moral arbitrariness.

Lack of transcendent orientation: Without a transcendent, personal God, the necessary external orientation beyond the relative world is lacking. This orientation is essential for establishing fixed and unchanging values that exist independently of cultural and individual preferences.

A personal God, on the other hand, offers clear and absolute moral standards that flow from His transcendent nature and His relationship with human beings. These values and standards are firmly established and provide a stable foundation that transcends the purely human. Belief in a personal God enables people to align themselves with a higher truth and live lives of meaning, purpose, and moral integrity.

The relationship between God and man:

The relationship between God and human beings is central to the understanding of a personal God. This relationship is characterized by love, responsibility, communication, and a deep sense of community. There are several key components that define this relationship and distinguish it from other spiritual concepts.

Divine Love and Care:

Divine love is at the heart of the relationship between God and man. God loves each person unconditionally and desires the best for His creation. This love is evident in God's care for humanity, His willingness to forgive, and His desire to establish a personal relationship with each individual. Divine love provides comfort, hope, and a deep sense of security.

Communication and Prayer:

Another essential aspect of the relationship between God and man is communication. God speaks to people through the scriptures, prophets, and inner promptings. In turn, people can communicate with God through prayer. Prayer allows believers to express their concerns, hopes, and gratitude, and provides an opportunity to receive divine guidance and wisdom. This two-way communication strengthens the relationship and deepens trust in God.

Divine Commandments and Human Responsibilities:

The relationship between God and man is also characterized by divine commandments and human responsibility. God has given mankind rules and commandments to guide them in living lives of moral integrity and fulfillment. These commandments are an expression of divine wisdom and love and provide clear guidelines for ethical behavior. Obeying these commandments is a form of obedience and respect for God.

Man has the responsibility to obey these commandments and to live according to divine principles. This responsibility is not only individual, but also collective. Each person contributes to the moral and spiritual health of the community by respecting and living the divine commandments.

To better illustrate the importance of these divine commandments, we would like to use the ten central commandments of the Judeo-Christian tradition as an example. These commandments have played a central role in the development of Western culture and ethics, providing a clear moral compass for living in accordance with divine principles.

The Ten Commandments:

1. I am the Lord, your God. You shall not have other gods besides me: This commandment emphasizes the uniqueness and exclusivity of faith in the one God and forbids the worship of other gods or idols.

2. You shall not take the name of the Lord, your God, in vain: The name of God is to be treated with reverence and respect, and you are to avoid using it frivolously or dishonestly.

3. Remember to keep holy the Lord's day.: The Sabbath is a day of rest and reflection on God. This commandment calls us to sanctify one day of the week and take a break from daily work to focus on spiritual things.

4. Honor your father and mother: This commandment emphasizes the importance of respecting and honoring one's parents and provides the foundation for strong family bonds.

5. Thou shalt not kill: This commandment prohibits the intentional killing of another human being and emphasizes the sanctity of human life.

6. Thou shalt not commit adultery: Adultery is forbidden to preserve the integrity and sanctity of marriage.

7. Thou shalt not steal: This commandment protects property rights and prohibits the theft or unlawful appropriation of another's property.

8. Thou shalt not bear false witness against your neighbor: Prohibits lying and bearing false witness against others, and promotes truth and justice in interpersonal relationships.

9. Thou shalt not covet your neighbor's wife: This commandment forbids envy and covetousness of another person's relationships, and promotes contentment and gratitude.

10. Thou shalt not covet your neighbor's goods: This expands on the previous commandment by prohibiting any coveting of another person's possessions or relationships.

These commandments provide a clear moral compass and help believers live lives in harmony with divine principles. By following these commandments, believers demonstrate their respect and obedience to God and contribute to the moral and spiritual health of their community.

Individual and Community Responsibility:

The relationship with God demands both individual and collective responsibility. Individually, each believer is called to live a life consistent with the divine commandments and to use his or her talents and abilities for the benefit of others. This includes ongoing personal development and the pursuit of moral integrity.

Collectively, this responsibility means that communities and societies should also live according to divine principles. A society guided by transcendent values promotes justice, compassion, and mutual respect. This collective responsibility strengthens social cohesion and creates a culture of trust and solidarity.

Divine Mercy and Forgiveness:

Another important aspect of the relationship between God and human beings is divine mercy and forgiveness. People make mistakes and sin, but God is ready to forgive when they repent and ask for forgiveness. This forgiveness is an expression of God's infinite mercy and offers people the opportunity to start afresh. It strengthens the relationship with God and gives believers the power to overcome their weaknesses and live a better life.

Eternal fellowship:

The relationship between God and human beings does not end with physical death. Many religious traditions teach that the relationship with God is eternal and that believers enter into a deeper communion with God after death. This perspective adds an extra dimension to earthly life and motivates believers to live according to divine commandments in order to achieve this eternal communion.

In summary, the relationship between God and man is a dynamic and living connection characterized by love, communication, responsibility, and mercy. This relationship provides direction, meaning, and hope, and enables people to live fulfilling lives of moral integrity.

Divine Commandments and Human Responsibilities:

Divine commandments are central to the relationship between God and humanity. They provide clear guidance and help believers live according to divine principles. These commandments are an expression of God's wisdom and love and serve as moral guidelines that shape people's behavior and decisions.

Orientation through divine commandments:

Divine commandments provide a firm moral framework that gives us direction in an often chaotic and relativistic world. They help us distinguish right from wrong and make ethical decisions. These commandments are not arbitrary, but are based on divine wisdom that has the good of all creation in mind.

An example of a divine commandment is the commandment to love our neighbor, which calls us to love our fellow human beings and to treat them with respect and compassion. Another example is the commandment to reverence God, which instructs us to honor God and obey His commandments. These and other commandments provide clear and reliable moral guidance that helps us live lives of integrity and fulfillment.

Man's Responsibility to God:

With the divine commandments comes man's responsibility to God. This responsibility has several dimensions:

Moral responsibility: Man has a moral obligation to obey the divine commandments and live his life according to God's principles. This means that we always consider the divine commandments in our decisions and actions, and strive to live a life in accordance with God's will.

Spiritual responsibility: In addition to moral responsibility, we also have a spiritual responsibility to maintain and deepen our relationship with God. This can be done through prayer, meditation, the study of scripture, and participation in religious communities. Spiritual responsibility helps us strengthen our connection with God and seek His guidance in our lives.

Social responsibility: The divine commandments also include responsibility to our fellow human beings and to the community. This means that we care not only for our own well-being, but also for the well-being of others. We are called to practice justice, compassion, and charity, and to work for the common good.

The believer's self-image as a creature:

A person who believes in a personal God sees himself or herself as a creature of that God. This understanding shapes their self-image and their relationship with God. In contrast to an atheist who sees himself as the result of an aimless evolutionary process and considers himself to be autonomous and independent, the believer recognizes his dependence on God. This dependence is not a limitation, but a natural consequence of creation. To believe in God is to accept that one does not exist by oneself, but has been created by a higher being. This understanding leads to a natural and self-evident recognition of divine commandments.

The Role of Divine Commandments in Society:

Divine commandments have not only individual but also collective significance. They serve as the foundation for the moral and ethical order of society. In a world characterized by relativism and moral arbitrariness, divine commandments provide a stable foundation upon which communities and societies can be built.

By adhering to the divine commandments, societies can promote justice, peace, and harmony. These precepts help to strengthen social structures and promote social cohesion. By respecting and living the divine commandments, we contribute to the creation of a just and compassionate society.

The importance of voluntary observance:

Another important aspect of the divine commandments is that their observance must be voluntary and of one's own free will. God has endowed human beings with free will, which means that we have the choice to obey or ignore His commandments. This freedom is an expression of divine love and a recognition of human autonomy.

Why God gave man free will:

God did not create slaves or human machines to blindly do his will. Instead, he created human beings in his image, as free individuals with their own consciousness and will. This freedom allows people to consciously and voluntarily choose God. God desires a personal relationship with His creatures, a relationship based on mutual love. Love can only exist on the basis of freedom; there is no love under compulsion. This freedom necessary for love is the deeper reason why God gave human beings free will.

Voluntary observance of the divine commandments demonstrates our respect and love for God. It is an expression of our desire to live according to His will and to deepen our relationship with Him. This voluntary devotion strengthens our moral integrity and spiritual growth.

In sum, the divine commandments provide clear moral guidance and contribute to the creation of a just and harmonious society. Man's responsibility to God encompasses moral, spiritual, and social dimensions and is manifested in the voluntary observance of these commandments. By following the divine commandments, we can live a fulfilled and meaningful life in harmony with God's will.

Individual and community responsibility:

Belief in a personal God strengthens both individual and collective responsibility. This dual responsibility is central to harmonious and just coexistence and promotes the moral and ethical integrity of both the individual and the community.

Individual responsibility:

Individual responsibility means that each person is accountable to God and to his or her fellow human beings for his or her own actions. Faith in God provides individuals with clear moral guidance and a strong sense of obligation to live according to God's commandments. This responsibility has several dimensions:

Moral Integrity: Faith in God encourages individuals to make decisions with moral integrity and to live a life consistent with divine principles. This includes honesty, justice, compassion, and respect for others.

Self-reflection and repentance: The faith encourages the practice of introspection and repentance. Believers are encouraged to regularly examine their own actions and admit mistakes. This leads to personal growth and a steady approach to divine ideals.

Responsibility for one's own actions: Each believer is aware that he or she is accountable to God for his or her actions. This realization encourages a conscious and responsible lifestyle.

Collective responsibility:

In addition to individual responsibility, belief in God also emphasizes collective responsibility. Communities and societies guided by divine principles promote social cohesion and the common good.

Sense of Community and Solidarity: Belief in God fosters a strong sense of community and solidarity among believers. This community supports its members in difficult times and works together to create a just and compassionate society.

Social Justice: Faith communities are committed to social justice. They engage in charitable projects, support those in need, and advocate for the rights of the oppressed. This collective responsibility contributes to the betterment of society and ensures that the divine principles of justice and mercy are realized in the world.

Caring for creation: Faith in God includes a responsibility to preserve and protect creation. Communities guided by divine principles are committed to protecting the environment and promoting sustainable lifestyles.

The interplay of individual and collective responsibility:

The interplay of individual and collective responsibility fosters a strong community characterized by moral integrity. Individuals who live according to godly principles contribute to the moral health of the community. At the same time, a community guided by godly values strengthens the individual growth and moral integrity of its members.

Practical Implementation:

Education and training: One practical expression of this responsibility is education and training based on godly principles. Religious communities place a high value on educating their children and youth in accordance with divine commandments and teaching them the importance of responsibility and moral integrity.

Religious practice: Religious practices such as prayer, worship, and community activities foster an awareness of individual and collective responsibility. These practices provide opportunities for self-reflection, community building, and working together for the common good.

Involvement and volunteerism: People of faith are often involved in charitable and volunteer activities. Through their involvement, they actively contribute to the betterment of society and embody the divine principles of charity and mercy.

In sum, belief in a personal God strengthens both individual and collective responsibility. By focusing on divine principles, believers promote moral integrity, social cohesion, and the common good. This dual responsibility is crucial to the creation of a just, compassionate, and harmonious society.

2.5 Practical application of faith

Integrating faith into everyday life:

Faith in God should not be a theoretical conviction, but should be manifested in daily life. Integrating faith into daily life means that the principles and values of the faith are actively lived and implemented in daily decisions and actions. There are several ways in which faith in God can be practiced in daily life:

Prayer and meditation:

Prayer is a central part of the life of faith and provides a way to communicate with God on a regular basis. Daily prayer times help to begin and end the day in harmony with God. Prayer allows people to express gratitude, ask for guidance and wisdom, and bring personal requests before God. Meditation can also be a valuable practice for finding inner peace and focusing on the presence of God.
Reading the Scriptures:

Regular reading and study of sacred scriptures helps to better understand and integrate divine principles and commandments into daily life. The scriptures offer wisdom, inspiration, and moral guidance that can be applied in everyday life. By reading the scriptures, one can delve deeper into the faith and build a stronger connection with God.

Participation in a religious community:

Participation in religious communities provides support and encouragement in the life of faith.

Shared worship, prayer groups, and religious events encourage interaction with other believers and strengthen a sense of community. Religious communities also provide opportunities for corporate worship, learning, and service to others.

Apply divine principles to daily actions:

The values and principles of faith should be evident in daily decisions and actions. This means acting with honesty, justice, and compassion in personal and professional relationships. Faith should be reflected in the way one treats others, resolves conflicts, and accepts responsibility.

Charity and Service to Others:

An important aspect of faith is charity, which is manifested in service to others. This can be done through volunteer work, charitable activities, and helping those in need. Service to others not only promotes the good of the community, but also strengthens one's faith and sense of fulfillment.

Ethical and moral decisions:

Faith in God provides clear moral guidelines for decision making. In everyday life, this means making choices that are consistent with God's commandments, even when they are difficult or unpopular. These choices promote personal integrity and contribute to a just and harmonious society.

Self-discipline and personal growth:

Faith in God encourages ongoing personal development and self-discipline. This can be done by setting spiritual goals, regular self-reflection, and finding ways to improve one's character. Personal development is an ongoing process supported by faith in God and keeping His commandments.

Gratitude and contentment:

The practice of gratitude is an essential part of the life of faith. Daily gratitude practices help to recognize the blessings in life and maintain a positive attitude. Gratitude fosters contentment and strengthens trust in God's care and plan for life.

Conscious lifestyle:

Faith in God encourages a conscious and mindful lifestyle. This means consciously reflecting on one's actions and choices and seeking ways to live one's life according to divine principles. A conscious lifestyle contributes to spiritual and moral development and promotes a fulfilled and meaningful life.

In summary, integrating faith into everyday life means actively living the principles and values of the faith and implementing them in daily decisions and actions. Through prayer, meditation, scripture reading, participation in religious communities, service to others, ethically pure activities, self-discipline, gratitude, and conscious living, faith in God can be anchored in everyday life and contribute to a fulfilled and meaningful life.

Strengthening Families and Communities:

Faith in God has an impact not only on the individual, but also on the collective. It can strengthen families and communities by promoting shared values and goals and by fostering social cohesion. These collective aspects of faith are critical to creating a just and compassionate society.

Shared values and goals:

Shared values and goals strengthen the cohesion of families and communities. Faith in God provides a clear and unchanging foundation for such values and goals. By aligning themselves with divine principles, families and communities can develop a common direction and understanding.

Foster cohesion: Shared values and goals promote cohesion within families and communities. They provide a common foundation upon which members can orient and rely. This creates a sense of belonging and cohesiveness.

Strengthen the family structure: Faith in God can strengthen the family structure by defining clear roles and responsibilities. Parents who actively live their faith provide moral guidance and a stable environment for their children. Shared religious practices, such as prayer and worship attendance, promote unity and understanding within the family.

Shared goals: Faith in God promotes common goals that transcend individual interests. These goals may include charitable projects, community events, or social initiatives. Such common endeavors strengthen the sense of community and encourage cooperation.

Support and cohesion:

Belief in God can support communities and strengthen social cohesion by promoting compassion, caring, and solidarity. These values are essential to the well-being of a community and help create a supportive and harmonicus environment. Promoting compassion and caring: Belief in God emphasizes the importance of compassion and caring for others. Faith communities are often active in helping those in need and advocating for social justice. These activities strengthen social cohesion and foster a culture of solidarity.

Creating networks of support: Faith communities create support networks to help members through difficult times. These networks provide emotional, spiritual, and practical support and help promote the well-being of community members.

Strengthening social cohesion: Belief in God can strengthen social cohesion by promoting shared rituals and practices. Shared worship, festivals and religious celebrations create opportunities for sharing and foster a stronger sense of community. These shared experiences promote a sense of belonging and help build strong social bonds.

Foster moral integrity: Communities guided by divine values promote moral integrity and ethical behavior. These values are critical to building trust and respect within the community. By setting moral examples and ethical standards, religious communities contribute to the creation of a just and harmonious society.

In sum, faith in God strengthens families and communities by promoting shared values and goals and fostering social cohesion. Guided by divine principles, communities can develop compassion, care, and solidarity, and create a supportive and harmonious environment. These collective aspects of faith are critical to creating a just and compassionate society.

Excursus: Misconduct in Churches and Religious Communities

For the sake of completeness, it should not go unmentioned that in the recent past churches and religious communities have been confronted with negative reports of immoral behavior, including cases of child abuse. These allegations must be taken seriously and require careful and transparent investigation. It is the responsibility of the churches not only to clarify such incidents, but also to ensure that they do not recur. It is a central part of ecclesial and religious ethics to face and learn from one's own misconduct.

The author of this book has not had such experiences in his personal experience, for example in church institutions and boarding schools. Nevertheless, the allegations and the possibility that such offenses may have occurred cannot be dismissed out of hand. The fact that human error and moral failure occur even within religious institutions is human nature and underscores the need for constant ethical self-examination.

However, these incidents should be viewed in the context of the modern and postmodern zeitgeist. In a society in which all values and norms are increasingly relativized and unconditional personal freedom is propagated as the highest good, churches and religious communities represent a countervailing force. They stand for absolute values and norms and represent the cause of the unchanging, transcendent God in the world He has created. For this reason, they are often the target of criticism and attacks aimed at undermining their moral authority.

It is conceivable that the constant repetition of these accusations and the associated negative press coverage may also be used in part to systematically damage the reputation of the churches. Such accusations are particularly effective because they directly challenge the credibility of institutions that are supposed to be moral models.

Finally, it should be emphasized that despite these challenges, churches and religious communities continue to play an indispensable role in representing God-given ethical principles and moral guidelines in society. The critical examination of one's own mistakes is not only necessary, but also an expression of the effort to come closer to the divine ideal. It is important that the faithful not be led astray from the path of faith by the misconduct of individuals, but that they orient themselves all the more toward the unchanging values established by God.

2.6 The Role of Holiness and Transcendence in the Life of Faith

Introduction:

God is transcendent and immanent, but never profane. Therefore, worship, invocation, and prayer must not be profane. Contact with God must always be something special and holy. The secular world has a tendency to profane everything, and the churches have an increasing tendency to profane worship services and Holy Mass. But this is counterproductive to faith and the development of faith. This chapter explains why holiness and transcendence are essential and how they can be maintained in the daily life of faith.

Importance of Holiness and Transcendence:

Holiness as the Core of Faith

Sacred spaces and times: Faith requires sacred spaces and times that are separate from the profanity of everyday life. Churches, cathedrals, and special times such as Sunday or religious holidays are examples of such sacred places and times.

Sacred Acts: Sacraments and rituals such as Holy Mass, baptism, or confirmation are expressions of holiness and should be performed with due respect and reverence.

Danger of profanation

Loss of Holiness: When religious acts and spaces are desecrated, faith loses depth and meaning. A profane perspective can impede access to transcendence and deep spiritual experience.

Everyday profanity: The constant mixing of the profane with the sacred can lead to a trivialization of faith, where believers no longer recognize the special meaning of their spiritual practices.

Practical tips for maintaining sanctity:
Mindfulness and Respect

Preparation for worship: Prepare inwardly for worship by intentionally taking time to quiet yourself and tune into your encounter with God.

Respectful participation: Participate in worship services and sacred ordinances with the reverence and attention they deserve. Avoid distractions and respect sacred spaces and times.

Prayer and Meditation

Pray reverently: Treat your prayer time as sacred. Find a quiet and respectful place to pray, and organize your prayer with deep devotion and seriousness. To further emphasize the sacredness of prayer, it may be helpful to create a "sacred place" in your home. This can be a small altar or a special corner where you place holy pictures, statues of saints, or a cross. Lighting a candle before praying can symbolize that you are entering a state of devotion and transcendence and connecting with the sacred world.

Meditation and Contemplation: Use meditation to focus on the sacredness and transcendence of God. This practice can help you better understand and live the difference between the profane and the sacred. The environment of your "sacred place" can also be a valuable support during meditation to deepen the spiritual atmosphere and strengthen your inner focus.

Education and Mediation

Religious education: Teach your children the importance of sanctity in the faith. Teach them to respect sacred actions and places and to recognize the transcendence of God.

Role modeling: Be a model of holiness yourself. Your own attitude and behavior can show others the importance of preserving the sacred in the life of faith.

Traditional Forces in the Catholic Church:

Traditionalist groups, especially in the Catholic Church, such as the Society of St. Pius X, the Society of St. Peter, and the Institute of Christ the King and High Priest, are particularly concerned with the permanent preservation of the holiness and trans-

99

cendence of the sacred elements of the Church, especially the Holy Mass. These communities celebrate Holy Mass in Latin according to the Tridentine Rite, which has been handed down for many centuries. This gives the celebration of the Mass a special and deliberately sacred atmosphere that points to the glory of God and his transcendence. These communities maintain parishes in many cities in Germany, Europe and around the world. There you can experience traditional Christian spirituality that is often not found in modern parishes. It is advisable to visit these places and communities from time to time to strengthen your faith and relationship with God.

Conclusion:

The preservation of holiness and transcendence is crucial to a deep and fulfilling life of faith. In a world that tends to profane everything, it is important to make a conscious effort to preserve and promote the sacred. This helps not only to deepen faith, but also to find a deeper connection to God and to make the spiritual journey authentic and meaningful.

2.7 Conclusion of the Chapter

Summary of key points:

In this chapter we have explored the possibility of a way out of the crisis of modern and postmodern societies through conscious belief in a personal God. The central arguments and insights are

Belief as a rational choice: We have argued that belief in a personal God can be a conscious and rational choice. Philosophical and scientific arguments support this belief and show that it provides a reasonable and sound basis.

Philosophical and Scientific Arguments: We have examined various philosophical arguments (cosmological argument, teleological argument) and scientific considerations (informational complexity of DNA, fine-tuning of the universe) that support belief in God.

Pragmatic Reasons: Belief in God provides numerous pragmatic benefits, including meaning and purpose in life, moral guidance, community and belonging, psychological well-being, and social responsibility.

Transcendent Values and Standards: We have emphasized the importance of transcendent values and norms that exist independently of cultural and individual preferences. These values provide a stable foundation for moral and ethical behavior and contrast with the relativity of the modern world.

Belief in a personal God: We have described the characteristics of a personal God and explained how the relationship between God and man is structured. This relationship is based on divine love, communication, commandments, and human responsibility.

Individual and Group Responsibility: Belief in God strengthens both individual and collective responsibility. This promotes the moral integrity of the individual and the social cohesion of the community.

Practical application of faith: We have explained how faith can be integrated into everyday life through prayer, meditation, reading the Scriptures, participation in religious communities, charity, and ethical decision-making.

Strengthening families and communities: Faith in God promotes shared values and goals that strengthen cohesion and solidarity within families and communities. Religious communities provide support and create a supportive and harmonious environment.

Finally, we have emphasized the role of holiness and transcendence in the life of faith and warned against turning faith and the relationship with God into something profane. God is transcendent and immanent, but never profane! He is holy and our relationship with him must always reflect this.

Moving on to practical examples and testimonies:

Having examined the theoretical foundations and practical implementation of belief in a personal God, in the next chapter we will present concrete examples and success stories. These stories will show how people and communities have integrated faith into their lives and the positive changes that have resulted.

We will share stories of individuals, families and communities who have successfully lived out their faith and overcome challenges. These examples will inspire and encourage people to actively integrate faith in God into their daily lives. They offer practical insights and show how the conscious act of faith can lead to a fulfilled and meaningful life.

Chapter 3:
Practical Examples and Inspiration

3.1 Introduction

Purpose and goal of this chapter:

In the previous chapters, we have comprehensively covered the theoretical foundations of belief in a personal God and the importance of transcendent values and standards. In this chapter, we want to encourage the reader to put theory into practice and show how faith can be lived out in daily life.

Practical examples and inspiration are essential to show that faith is not just about abstract concepts, but can have concrete, life-changing effects. By sharing real stories of individuals and families, we want to show how faith in God has sustained, strengthened and inspired people in different life situations. These examples are meant to encourage and show that it is possible to actively integrate faith into one's life and experience positive change in the process.

Overview of upcoming content:

This chapter is divided into several sections that highlight different aspects of putting faith into practice:

Return Experiences and Personal Transformations: Here we share inspiring stories of individuals and families who have experienced profound changes in their lives through their intentional faith in God. These stories show how faith can help people overcome personal crises and lead more fulfilling lives.

Principles and Practices for Everyday Life: In this section, we present various spiritual practices and principles that can help people live out their faith in everyday life. These include prayer and meditation, common religious rituals, and ethical and moral guidelines.

Community and support: Faith is often lived and strengthened in community. Here we look at the role of religious communities, the support and sense of belonging they provide, and examples of community involvement and social projects.
Reflection and Application: At the end of the chapter, we will summarize the key lessons and insights and provide practical tips on how to apply the principles and examples presented in your own life.

Through this structure, we hope to not only inform, but also inspire and motivate the reader to actively live out their faith and experience the positive changes that can result. The following sections detail how faith in God can be put into practice in various areas of life.

3.2 Returns and Personal Transformation

Conscious faith in God can profoundly change a person's life. Here are some inspiring stories of people who have experienced significant change through their conversion to faith.

- C.S. Lewis, a distinguished writer and theologian, was originally a staunch atheist. His journey to Christianity began with deep philosophical and spiritual questions that he could not ignore. In his book "Surprised by Joy," Lewis describes his conversion experience and how faith changed his life. He found comfort and meaning in the Christian faith and dedicated the rest of his life to spreading his beliefs through his writings and lectures.

- St. Augustine, one of the most influential church fathers, led a long life of dissipation, seeking truth in various philosophical doctrines.

His conversion to Christianity, which he describes in his "Confessions," was a turning point in his life. By the grace of God, Augustine found faith and dedicated his life to the Church. His writings and theological insights continue to shape Christianity today.

- John Newton, author of the famous hymn "Amazing Grace," was once a slave trader. His conversion to Christianity was a profound experience that led him to radically change his life. Newton came to see the wrongness of slavery and worked to abolish it. His story is a powerful testament to the transformative power of faith and the possibility of forgiveness and renewal.

- Lee Strobel, an award-winning journalist and committed atheist, set out to disprove the Christian faith. But his intense research led to his own conversion, which he chronicles in The Case for Jesus. Strobel found faith through his research and dedicated his life to defending the Christian faith. His story shows how intellectual honesty and the search for truth can lead to faith.

- Nicky Cruz, a violent gang leader in New York, experienced a dramatic conversion through an encounter with Christian evangelist David Wilkerson. His story, told in the book "Run Baby Run," demonstrates the transforming power of faith. Cruz found new meaning and purpose through faith and dedicated his life to working with at-risk youth and spreading the Gospel.

- Ayaan Hirsi Ali, a prominent critic of Islam and former atheist, recently publicly announced her faith in Christianity. Her conversion is notable because she previously worked closely with prominent atheists such as Richard Dawkins and Christopher Hitchens. Hirsi Ali explained that her decision to become a Christian had both spiritual and cultural reasons. She sees Christianity as a source of values and traditions that have strengthened Western civilization. Her conversion was a conscious choice driven by her desire to find a meaningful and unifying foundation for her life and society.

- Tammy Peterson, wife of renowned psychologist and author Jordan B. Peterson, experienced her conversion to Christianity in the wake of a serious illness. In the midst of her health crisis, Tammy found comfort and meaning in the Christian faith. Her husband, Jordan Peterson, has spoken in several interviews about the impact of Christian faith on their family and how they faced the illness together. Tammy Peterson's conversion was a profound personal transformation that gave her support and hope during an extremely difficult time.

- Eva Vlaardingerbroek, a Dutch political commentator and activist, found the Catholic faith during the COVID pandemic. Her conversion was the result of an intense spiritual search. She was particularly attracted to the doctrine of transubstantiation, which she had previously rejected as a Protestant. Her conversion took place during a Christmas Mass and had a strong influence on her political and social activism. For Eva, faith is not just a personal matter, but a driving force behind her work as a political commentator and activist.

- The author himself can also speak about how he found his way back to the God of Christianity, the Christian Church, and the Christian tradition after decades away from the Christian Church. Although he was baptized and raised as a Christian, as a young man he turned his back on the Church and the Christian religion, following the spirit of the times and seeking the meaning of life in esoteric practices, Far Eastern philosophies and other doctrines of salvation. He even wrote books on yoga and Vedanta, reincarnation techniques, and Central American sorcerers.

One day, however, while attending a spiritual event in the temple of a Far Eastern religious community, he suddenly realized with all his might that he was out of place there. As a baptized Christian and a person socialized in the Christian tradition, he did not really feel at home in a Far Eastern cult. Despite his intellectual knowledge of the rites and religious content practiced there, he had no inner, spiritual or cultural access to it.

This realization led him to leave the event, return home, and rejoin the Christian Church he had left as a young man. His return to God felt and still feels like the parable of the prodigal son described by Jesus Christ in the New Testament. It was like coming home - finally, after a long time and a long search, he had reached his destination.

These stories illustrate how intentional faith in God can profoundly change lives. They offer inspiring examples of the transforming power of faith and encourage us to actively live out our own faith.

3.3 Principles and Practices for Daily Life

Prayer and Meditation

The role of prayer and meditation in daily life:

Prayer and meditation are central practices in the daily life of a believer. They not only provide moments of peace and reflection, but also help to find a deeper connection with God and a clear direction in daily life. Through prayer, the believer opens a dialogue with God, expressing gratitude, petitions, and reflections. Daily prayer helps to resolve inner conflicts and to find comfort in difficult times.

Examples of practice:

Morning prayer: Begin the day with a short prayer to express gratitude for life and the tasks ahead. The "Our Father" or "Hail Mary" are traditional prayers that can set a spiritual tone for the day.

Noon meditation: Take a moment in the middle of the day for a short meditation. This can help clear the mind and focus on what is important.
The "Angelus," prayed three times a day in traditional Christianity, is a wonderful way to focus on God.

Evening Prayer: End the day with an evening prayer in which you reflect on the day, express gratitude for your experiences, and ask for guidance for the next day. The "rosary" offers a profound and meditative way to end the day in prayer.

Table Prayer: Saying a short prayer of thanksgiving before meals, such as "Come, Lord Jesus, be our guest and bless what you have given us," is a simple practice of thanking God for his gifts and integrating him into daily life.

Shared Religious Rituals

How Shared Religious Practices Strengthen Families and Communities
Shared religious rituals play an important role in strengthening families and communities. These rituals foster a sense of belonging and common purpose. Sharing religious experiences and practices deepens the spiritual bond within the family and community.

Examples of rituals include

Family devotions: Regular family devotions strengthen spiritual unity and provide an opportunity to talk about matters of faith. Praying the "rosary" together can be a profound spiritual experience and a means of strengthening family bonds.

Parish events: Attending church services, Bible study groups, and other parish activities builds a sense of community and provides support from the faith community.

Celebrating religious holidays: Celebrating holidays such as Christmas, Easter, or Pentecost together strengthens family and community bonds and provides an opportunity to reflect on faith and its meaning in daily life. In the Catholic calendar, there are many other feasts in honor of saints and the Virgin Mary, such as the Marian month of May, when regular Marian devotions are held.

Ethics and Morals in Daily Life

The importance of ethical and moral principles in everyday life:
Ethical and moral principles are essential for a well-ordered and meaningful life. Faith in God provides a firm foundation for these principles and helps us live them consistently in everyday life. By following God's commandments and teachings, the believer can act ethically and set an example for others.

Examples of principles:

Charity: Practice charity by treating others with compassion, respect, and a willingness to help. This can be done through small gestures of kindness, as well as through volunteering and assisting those in need.

Honesty and Integrity: Live by the principles of honesty and integrity by being transparent and sincere in all your actions and decisions. This builds trust and respect in your social and professional relationships.

Forgiveness: Practice forgiveness toward those who have wronged you. This not only frees you from negative feelings, but also promotes peace and reconciliation in your community.

Note: A small selection of traditional Christian prayers and devotions can be found in chapter 4 below. These prayers can help shape your daily spiritual life and deepen your connection with God.

These principles and practices offer concrete ways to integrate and live out your faith in everyday life. They not only help cultivate a deeper spiritual connection with God, but also strengthen family and community bonds and promote ethical and moral living.

3.4 Community and Support

Role of the Community

How participation in a religious community provides support and a sense of community:
Participation in a religious community offers many
benefits that go far beyond the purely spiritual. Religious communities provide a strong sense of belonging and cohesion. They serve as support networks that help members through difficult times
and navigate everyday life. Within the community,
friendships and relationships are formed that often
last a lifetime.

Exemplary aspects:

Shared worship: Regular attendance at worship services builds a sense of community and provides an
opportunity to pray and celebrate together.

Pastoral care: Religious communities offer pastoral
support from pastors, priests, and other spiritual
leaders. This support can take the form of conver-
sation, prayer, and practical help.

Educational programs: Many congregations offer
religious education programs such as Bible studies,
faith courses, and lectures that deepen faith and
broaden religious knowledge.

Social projects and outreach

Examples of faith-inspired social projects and involvement:
Religious communities are often very active in community service and helping those in need. Inspired by their faith, members engage in various social projects that promote the well-being of the community and society as a whole.

Exemplary projects:

Soup kitchens and food banks: Many churches operate soup kitchens and food banks that provide groceries and hot meals to those in need. These projects are often supported by volunteers who donate their time and resources.

Refugee relief: Religious communities are often involved in assisting refugees and immigrants. They offer language classes, legal services, and practical assistance to help newcomers integrate.

Helping the homeless: Churches and religious organizations provide shelter, medical care, and counseling to the homeless. These initiatives aim to provide hope and support to those in need.

Excursus: Abuse of charity by secular forces

We recognize that Christian principles of charity and helping those in need can sometimes be used within broader political and social agendas that are not always consistent with fundamental Christian values. In particular, issues such as aid to refugees and support for migrants are often discussed in political debates and can be used to advocate for policies that encourage unrestricted immigration, potentially leading to social tensions and challenges in host countries.

However, these abuses should not lead to questioning or devaluing fundamental Christian values and acts of charity. Christian charity remains a central imperative of our faith, which remains valid regardless of political and social abuses. However, it is important to understand and practice charity in the right context.

Our neighbor is not only the stranger, but also the person in our immediate environment - our neighbors, our friends, our families. Christian aid should always aim to provide concrete, direct assistance in accordance with Christian values and commandments. This means caring for those who literally "cross our path", who live in our immediate environment and need our immediate help.

Christian charity remains important and essential, but it should always be done thoughtfully and in balance with the needs of our own community and society. This is the only way to ensure that charity is not abused, but fulfills its true purpose - unconditional help to those who truly need it, in accordance with God's commandments.

Community Experiences

Testimonials from parishioners about their experiences and the support they have received from the parish:

Testimonials from parishioners show how significant and helpful support within a religious community can be. Here are a few examples:

Brian Birdwell: Brian was in the Pentagon when it was hit by a plane on September 11, 2001. With severe burns over 60% of his body, he barely survived and had to undergo nearly 40 reconstructive surgeries. Through the support of his community and his faith, Brian found the strength to carry on and eventually be elected to the Texas Senate.

Tyrone Flowers: After a shooting that left him a quadriplegic, Tyrone chose to forgive his attacker instead of seeking revenge. He found peace and understanding through his faith and is now dedicated to helping others in difficult circumstances.

Example from Germany: A family from Bavaria, Germany, shares how they found their way back to life after a serious car accident thanks to the support of their church. The church organized not only financial support, but also daily visits, help with childcare and prayer circles that gave the family strength and comfort.

These stories show how powerful the support of a religious community can be. The connection to a community offers not only spiritual but also practical help and strengthens the sense of belonging and cohesion.

These principles and examples illustrate the important role that religious communities can play in the lives of their members. They offer not only spiritual support, but also practical help and a strong sense of community that is invaluable in difficult times.

3.5 Reflection and Application

Keys to success

Analyze the factors that contributed to the success
of the stories presented:
The success stories and positive changes in the lives
of the individuals and communities described can
be traced back to certain key principles. These principles are universally applicable and provide a solid
foundation for one's own spiritual and practical life
journey.

Key Principles:

Faith and Trust: Unwavering faith in God and trust
in His guidance were central elements in all the success stories. This trust helped people persevere and
find comfort in difficult times.

Community and Support: The support of a religious
community played a critical role. This community
provided not only spiritual, but also emotional and
practical support, which contributed significantly to
success.

Active engagement: A willingness to get involved
and put faith into action was another key to success. Whether through volunteer work, participation in community activities, or personal prayer and

ritual, active engagement strengthened faith and community.

Forgiveness and charity: The principle of forgiveness and charity was present in many stories. These principles helped people find peace and heal relationships.

Applicable Principles

Identify principles and practices that readers can apply to their own lives:
The key principles mentioned can be applied in your own life in a variety of ways. Here are a few specific suggestions:

Faith and trust:

Daily prayer: Incorporate prayer into your daily routine. Begin and end your day with a prayer to strengthen your relationship with God and find direction.

Meditation and reflection: Set aside regular time for quiet meditation and reflection to find inner peace and clarity.

Community and support:

Attend community events: Get involved in your religious community. Attend worship services, Bible study groups, and other community events regularly for support and fellowship.

Volunteer: Get involved in community service projects and volunteer work. This not only strengthens the community, but also gives you a sense of making a positive contribution.

Active engagement:

Personal Rituals: Develop personal rituals that strengthen your faith and spirituality. This may include praying the rosary regularly, reading scripture, or celebrating religious holidays.

Education and Formation: Take advantage of educational opportunities in your community to deepen your faith and grow spiritually.

Forgiveness and charity:

Practice forgiveness: Practice forgiving others, even when it is difficult. Forgiveness frees you from negative feelings and promotes inner peace.

Be Compassionate: Show compassion and charity in your daily life. Small acts of kindness can make a big difference.

Encouragement for personal action

Motivation and practical tips on how readers can apply the insights and examples to their own daily lives:

Implementing these principles in your own life requires conscious choice and commitment. Here are some practical tips to help you integrate these principles into your daily life:

A step-by-step guide:

Set clear goals: Think about the spiritual and practical goals you want to achieve. Write down these goals and pursue them consistently.
Establish regular times for prayer and meditation: Incorporate regular times for prayer and meditation into your daily routine. This will help establish a regular practice.

Seek community: Join a religious community and actively participate in its activities. Support and interaction with other believers can help strengthen your faith.

Get socially involved: Find a way to be socially involved, whether through volunteering or supporting projects in your community.
Be patient and consistent: Integrating these principles into your daily life takes time and patience. Stay consistent and don't give up, even when challenges arise.

Inspirational quotes:

"Faith is the first step, even if you can't see all the way." - This quote reminds us that faith often begins with small steps.

"Forgiveness is the key to inner peace." - Forgiveness is a central principle that leads to inner peace and healing.

"Nothing should frighten you, nothing should scare you. Everything will pass. God alone remains the same. Everything is achieved by the patient, and whoever has God has everything. God alone is enough." - St. Teresa of Avila. This prayer emphasizes the constancy of God and the importance of trust and patience.

This reflection and application of the principles and practices can help you to apply the insights presented in this book to your own life and thereby experience spiritual and practical success.

3.6 Conclusion of the Chapter

Summary of the main points:
In this chapter, we have discussed in detail the importance and practical application of faith in daily life. We have used real-life success stories and concrete examples to illustrate how conscious faith in God can lead to positive change. Here are the key takeaways:

Experiences of return and personal transformation: The testimonies of people who have experienced profound changes in their lives through faith demonstrate the transformative power of faith.

Principles and Practices for Daily Living: We have presented practical principles and rituals that can integrate and strengthen faith in everyday life. These include prayer, meditation, shared religious rituals, and adherence to ethical and moral principles.

Community and Support: The role of religious community as a source of support and a sense of community was emphasized. Authentic testimonies showed how meaningful these communities can be in difficult times.

Reflection and application: We identified the key principles that contributed to the success of the stories presented and provided practical tips on how to apply these principles in our own lives.

Moving on to the next chapter:

In the next chapter, we will explore more advanced topics that deepen and strengthen faith in everyday life. We will look at specific challenges that may arise in the life of faith and provide practical guidance on how to overcome these challenges. We will also look at other spiritual practices and resources that can help you strengthen your faith and continue your spiritual journey.

Chapter 4:
Practical Application of Faith in Daily Life

4.1 Introduction

Purpose and goal of the chapter:

The fourth chapter is devoted to the practical application of faith in everyday life. The goal is to provide readers with concrete ways to live and integrate their faith on a daily basis. While the previous chapters dealt with the theoretical foundations and inspiring stories, this chapter offers practical instructions and tips. It is designed to help readers integrate the principles of faith into their personal, family, professional, and community contexts.

Overview of upcoming content:

This chapter is divided into four main areas, each addressing specific aspects of putting faith into practice:

Personal Spiritual Practices:
Different forms of prayer and meditation and their role in daily life.
Tips and examples for daily devotions and Bible reading.

The importance of gratitude and self-reflection in daily life.

Faith and Family:
Principles and practices for teaching faith to children.
Examples of religious rituals and traditions in the family.
How faith can help resolve family conflicts.

Faith and Work:
Applying Christian principles in the workplace.
Strategies for integrating faith and work.
How to live out and share your faith at work.

Faith and community:
The importance of participating in community events and worship.
Examples and suggestions for community-based social projects and mission work.
How to use your faith to help others in the community.

The chapter ends with a summary of key points and a look ahead to the next chapter, which will cover additional topics and practical instructions.

4.2 Personal Spiritual Practices

Prayer and Meditation

Prayer and meditation are central to the spiritual life. They provide moments of peace, reflection, and connection with God. Various forms of prayer and meditation can be incorporated into daily life to clear the mind and foster a deeper spiritual connection.

The importance of prayer:

Prayer is a way of communicating with God. It allows us to express our thoughts, concerns, gratitude, and requests. Praying regularly can help us find inner peace, gain spiritual clarity, and develop a closer relationship with God. Prayer is an act of respect and reverence for God. It is an opportunity to give thanks and praise to God for His gifts. Prayer strengthens our connection with God and gives us the confidence and trust we need in our daily lives.

Another important aspect of prayer is that it helps to transform consciously practiced faith into deeply felt conviction. Regular prayer develops a sense of security and trust in God. This connection promotes inner strength and confidence, which in turn can have a positive influence on our worldly life and success.

Examples of prayers:

The Lord's Prayer

Our Father, who art in heaven,
Hallowed be thy name.
Thy kingdom come.
Thy will be done,
on earth as it is in heaven.
Give us this day our daily bread.
And forgive us our trespasses,
as we forgive those who have trespassed
against us.
And lead us not into temptation,
But deliver us from evil.
Amen.

The Lord's Prayer, also known as the "Pater Noster", is the central prayer of Christianity, taught by Jesus Christ Himself. It is found in the Gospels of the New Testament, both in the Gospel of Matthew (Matthew 6:9-13) and in the Gospel of Luke (Luke 11:2-4). In the Bible, the prayer appears in the context of the Sermon on the Mount, where Jesus teaches his disciples how to pray.

The Lord's Prayer is not only a prayer, but also a summary of the essential beliefs of Christianity. It begins by addressing God as Father, emphasizing the close and personal relationship between God and believers. The prayer includes requests for the sanctification of God's name, the coming of His kingdom, the fulfillment of His will, daily provision, forgiveness of sins, and protection from temptation and evil.

The prayer has deep roots in Jewish tradition and reflects many elements of Jewish prayers in use at the time of Jesus. The "Our Father" is an expression of the intimate relationship between God and man, similar to that used in several Psalms and other Jewish texts.

Over the centuries, the Lord's Prayer has come to play a central role in the Christian liturgy and in personal prayer. It is recited in all Christian denominations and is considered the most fundamental and widespread prayer in Christianity. It serves not only as a model for prayer, but also as an expression of faith and devotion to God.

Glory be to the Father:

Glory be to the Father
and to the Son
and to the Holy Spirit,

as it was in the beginning,
is now and ever shall be,
world without end.
Amen.

The "Glory be to the Father" or "Gloria Patri" is a short doxology often used in the Christian tradition to praise the Holy Trinity - the Father, the Son, and the Holy Spirit. It has a central role in many Christian liturgies, and is often recited at the end of psalms or periods of prayer.

The "Glory be to the Father" comes from the early Christian church and is a simple but powerful praise of the Trinity of God. It has been prayed regularly for centuries in many denominations, including the Catholic, Orthodox, and Anglican churches. The words of the prayer summarize the central Christian belief that God exists in three persons: Father, Son, and Holy Spirit.

This prayer is used especially frequently in the Catholic Church's Liturgy of the Hours (the Officium), and is also deeply rooted in the Orthodox and Anglican traditions. It serves as a solemn conclusion to the prayers and psalms recited in the liturgy, reminding the faithful that all prayers are ultimately addressed to the Holy Trinity.

Overall, "Glory be to the Father' emphasizes the eternity and unchanging nature of God and is a brief but powerful invocation of the Trinity that inspires deep reverence and devotion in the faithful.

Glory to God in the highest (Gloria in excelsis Deo):

Glory to God in the highest,
and on earth peace to His people of good will.

We praise you,
we bless you,
we adore you,
we glorify you,
we give you thanks for your great glory,
Lord God, heavenly King,
O God, almighty Father.

Lord Jesus Christ, Only Begotten Son,
Lord God, Lamb of God, Son of the Father,
You take away the sins of the world:
have mercy on us;
you take away the sins of the world,
receive our prayer;
You are seated at the right hand of the Father,
have mercy on us.

For You alone are the Holy One,
You alone are the Lord,
You alone are the Most High,
Jesus Christ,
together with the Holy Spirit,
in the glory of God the Father.

Amen.

The prayer "Glory to God in the highest," or in Latin, "Gloria in excelsis Deo," is one of the oldest and most familiar hymns in Christian liturgy, especially in the Catholic Church. Usually sung or spoken during Mass, the Gloria is a hymn of praise that proclaims the glory of God and peace on earth. The prayer has its roots in the angelic song described in the Bible in the Gospel of Luke (Luke 2:14), when the angels sang at the birth of Jesus: "Glory to God in the highest, and on earth peace, goodwill to men."

The Gloria, which includes the phrase "Glory to God in the highest," is used especially on feast days and Sundays during Mass to express the congregation's joy and gratitude to God. It comes immediately after the Kyrie and before the Scripture readings in the liturgy, and is a solemn prelude to the rest of the service.

The text of the Gloria, including "Glory to God in the highest," is characterized by profound praise and is one of the central elements of Catholic and other Christian worship services. It reminds the faithful of the glory of God and the importance of peace and grace in their lives.

Hail Mary (Ave Maria):

Hail, Mary, full of grace,
the Lord is with thee.
Blessed art thou amongst women
and blessed is the fruit of thy womb, Jesus.
Holy Mary, Mother of God,
pray for us sinners,
now and at the hour of our death.
Amen.

The Ave Maria, also known as the "Hail Mary," is a central part of Catholic prayer life and is deeply rooted in Christian tradition. It is a prayer addressed directly to the Virgin Mary, the mother of Jesus, asking for her intercession.

The text of the Ave Maria is divided into two parts. The first part is based directly on biblical texts. The first words, "Hail Mary, full of grace, the Lord is with you" are taken from the Gospel of Luke (Luke 1:28), where the Archangel Gabriel speaks these words to Mary at the Annunciation. The next phrase, "You are blessed among women, and blessed is the fruit of your womb, Jesus," comes from Elizabeth, Mary's cousin, who greeted her in this way when she visited her (Luke 1:42).

The second part of the prayer, "Holy Mary, Mother of God, pray for us sinners, now and at the hour of our death," was added later by the Church and reflects the deep devotion and trust of the faithful in Mary's intercession.

The Hail Mary is often used in the Rosary, one of the most important prayers in the Catholic faith. It also serves as an expression of Marian devotion, which plays a special role in Catholicism. Many believers turn to Mary in times of need, trusting that she, as the mother of Jesus, will intercede for them before God.

The Hail Mary has united the faithful throughout the centuries and is a prayer that embodies consolation, hope and deep faith in the intercession of the Virgin Mary.

The Apostles' Creed:

I believe in God,
the Father almighty,
Creator of heaven and earth,
and in Jesus Christ, his only Son, our Lord,
who was conceived by the Holy Spirit,
born of the Virgin Mary,
suffered under Pontius Pilate,
was crucified, died and was buried;
he descended into hell;
on the third day he rose again from the dead;
he ascended into heaven,
and is seated at the right hand of God
the Father almighty;
from there he will come to judge the living
and the dead.
I believe in the Holy Spirit,
the holy catholic Church,
the communion of saints,
the forgiveness of sins,
the resurrection of the body,
and life everlasting.

Amen.

The Apostles' Creed, also known as the Nicene Creed, is one of the oldest and most important creeds in Christianity. It serves as a concise summary of the essential beliefs shared by all Christians, regardless of their denomination. Outside the Catholic Church, the phrase: "I believe in ..., the Holy Catholic Church ..." is usually replaced by the phrase: "I believe in ..., the Holy Christian Church ...".

The Creed dates back to the early Church and is traditionally attributed to the apostles, although it was not fully formulated in its present form until the 4th century. It summarizes the teachings of the apostles on the nature of God, Jesus Christ, and the Holy Spirit, and expresses belief in the Trinity.

The Apostles' Creed has special significance in Catholic and Protestant Christianity and is used in many church services and liturgical acts, especially at baptisms and as part of daily prayers, such as morning and evening prayers.

The text of the Confession is divided into three sections, each dealing with an aspect of the Trinity:

1. belief in God the Father: "I believe in God the Father, the Almighty, the Creator of heaven and earth."

2. Faith in Jesus Christ: This section describes the life, death, resurrection, and future return of Jesus Christ.

3. Faith in the Holy Spirit: This section deals with the role of the Holy Spirit, the Church, the communion of saints, the forgiveness of sins, and eternal life.

The Apostles' Creed is not only an expression of personal faith, but also a confession of the fellowship of all believers united in these central truths of faith. It is a symbol of the unity and continuity of Christian doctrine handed down from the earliest days of the Church to the present day.

Practical tips for incorporating prayer into your daily life:

Morning prayer: Begin the day with prayer as soon as you get up, before you plunge into the hustle and bustle of everyday life. The "Our Father" or "Hail Mary" can help you set a spiritual tone for the day. This practice creates a spiritual foundation for the day and promotes a sense of calm and peace.

Noontime prayer: Use your lunch hour for a short prayer or meditation. The "Angelus" prayer (see below) is traditionally said at noon, often as the church bells ring. It is a wonderful way to stop the day and focus on God. It helps to take a spiritual break in the midst of daily tasks.

Evening prayer: Evening is a great time to end the day with prayer. Praying the Rosary (see below) can be a meditative practice that helps you reflect on the day and end it in peace. This practice can be done alone, with the family, or in communities such as Radio Maria.

Daily devotions

Regular devotions and the reading of religious texts are essential to daily spiritual practice. Devotions often consist of a set series of prayers, which may be supplemented by psalms, hymns, and scripture readings. A devotional may also include meditations, reflections, and personal prayers that focus on the life of Jesus Christ, the saints, or specific truths of the faith. These elements are offered in a quiet and contemplative atmosphere, often accompanied by candlelight or other symbols that emphasize the sacredness and transcendence of the prayer time. Devotions are designed to bring the faithful closer to God, to deepen their faith, and to provide a time of inner reflection and peace. They provide an opportunity for daily reflection on God's Word and spiritual nourishment. Here are two examples of common daily devotions:

The Angel of the Lord (The Angelus):

The Angel of the Lord declared unto Mary,
And she conceived by the Holy Spirit.

Hail Mary, full of grace,
The Lord is with you;
Blessed art thou among women,
and blessed is the fruit of thy womb, Jesus.
Holy Mary, Mother of God,
pray for us sinners,
now and at the hour of our death. Amen.

Behold the handmaid of the Lord,
Be it done unto me according to your word.

Hail Mary, full of grace,
The Lord is with you;
Blessed art thou among women,
and blessed is the fruit of thy womb, Jesus.
Holy Mary, Mother of God,
pray for us sinners,
now and at the hour of our death. Amen.

And the Word became flesh,
and dwelt among us.

Hail Mary, full of grace,
The Lord is with you;
Blessed art thou among women,
and blessed is the fruit of thy womb, Jesus.
Holy Mary, Mother of God,
pray for us sinners,
now and at the hour of our death. Amen.

Pray for us, O Holy Mother of God,
that we may be made worthy of the promises of
Christ.

Let us pray;

Pour forth, we beseech you, O Lord,
your grace into our hearts:
that we, to whom the Incarnation of Christ
your Son was made known by the message
of an Angel,
may be brought by his Passion and Cross
to the glory of his Resurrection.
Through the same Christ our Lord.

Amen

The Angelus is a traditional Catholic devotional prayer that recalls the Annunciation of the Lord to the Virgin Mary by the Archangel Gabriel, as described in the Gospel of Luke (Luke 1:26-38). The name "Angelus" comes from the first words of the Latin text: "Angelus Domini nuntiavit Mariae", which means: "The Angel of the Lord brought the message to Mary".

This prayer was developed as a form of devotion in the 11th century and quickly spread throughout the Western Church. It is traditionally prayed three times a day: morning, noon, and evening, often in conjunction with the ringing of church bells to remind the faithful to pause and reflect on the meaning of God's incarnation in Jesus Christ.

The Angelus consists of three short biblical quotations, each of which is followed by an Ave Maria and a concluding petition. The structure and content of the prayer are designed to remind the faithful of the central Christian mystery of the Incarnation and to lead them into an attitude of humility and faith.

In many Catholic communities and families, the Angelus is still practiced today as an integral part of daily prayer, contributing to spiritual deepening by calling the faithful to reflection and prayer three times a day.

The Rosary:

The Rosary is a traditional Catholic form of devotion and prayer that focuses on meditating on the most important events in the lives of Jesus Christ and the Virgin Mary. The name "rosary" is derived from the prayer chain used for the prayer, combined with the idea that each bead of this chain, each representing a prayer, is like a rose offered to Mary, the mother of Jesus. In its practical application, therefore, the Rosary is a circular prayer chain consisting of 59 beads and an attached cross, which structure the prayer and guide the person praying.

The Rosary consists of several prayers that are said in a fixed order. These prayers are

1. The Sign of the Cross: One begins with the Sign of the Cross to place oneself in the presence of God. To do this, touch your forehead, chest, left shoulder, and right shoulder with your right hand in that order and say: In the name of the Father and of the Son and of the Holy Spirit, Amen.

2. The Apostles' Creed: It is prayed at the cross and confesses the Christian faith. (Text, see above)

2. The Lord's Prayer: It follows the Creed and is prayed at the first large bead of the Rosary. (Text, see above)

3. Three Hail Marys (text, see above): These are prayed at the next three small beads, usually as a petition for faith, hope, and charity, the three central Christian virtues.

4 Glory be to the Father: This is prayed after the three Hail Marys. (Text, see above)

5. The main part of the rosary consists of five decades (sections), each decade consisting of 11 beads, one "Our Father" and ten "Hail Marys", followed by a "Glory be to the Father".

While saying these prayers, one meditates on a "mystery" - a significant event in the life of Jesus or Mary.

The Rosary is traditionally divided into three "decades", each of which contains five "mysteries":

1. The Joyful Mysteries (Joyful Rosary):

- The Annunciation of the Lord to Mary
- Mary's visit to her cousin Elizabeth
- The birth of Jesus in Bethlehem
- The Presentation of Jesus in the Temple
- The Twelve-Year-Old Jesus in the Temple

2. The Sorrowful Mysteries (Sorrowful Rosary)

- The agony in the Garden
- The scourging of Jesus at the pillar
- The crowning of Jesus with thorns
- Jesus carrying the cross
- The Crucifixion of Jesus

3. The Glorious Mysteries (Glorious Rosary)

- The Resurrection of Jesus from the Dead
- The Ascension of Jesus into Heaven
- The Descent of the Holy Spirit
- The Assumption of Mary into Heaven
- The Coronation of Mary as Queen of Heaven

The Rosary can be prayed alone or with others. In groups, the Rosary is often prayed in alternation: One person says the first half of each prayer (e.g., "Hail Mary, full of grace...") and the others say the second half ("Hail Mary, Mother of God, pray for us sinners..."). The meditation on the mysteries is done in silence and is announced before each decade.

A final prayer to Mary is often added at the end of the Rosary. For example, the oldest known Marian prayer ("Sub tuum praesidium") dates from the third century:

We fly to your protection

We fly to your protection,
O holy Mother of God;
Do not despise our petitions in our need,
but always deliver us from all dangers,
O glorious and blessed Virgin.
Amen.

The Rosary typically concludes with the sign of the cross.

The Rosary is not only a form of prayer, but also a meditative path that helps the faithful to better understand and venerate the life of Christ and the role of Mary in salvation.

Thus, the Rosary is a meditative path of prayer that promotes a deeper spiritual connection through the persistent repetition of the prayers. The average length of time spent praying one of the three decades of the Rosary is about half an hour. The entire Rosary, including all three decades, takes about an hour and a half.

Praying the Rosary together in Christian families and groups is very popular because it can be a profound spiritual experience. Christian radio stations, such as Radio Maria, offer worldwide "live" or "online" Rosary prayers in all languages, in which listeners can participate directly "on air" and thus form a large prayer community.

Gratitude and reflection

Gratitude and reflection are important elements in the daily life of the faithful. These practices help focus on the positive and recognize God's blessings in everyday life.

Gratitude journal: Keep a journal in which you write down three things for which you are grateful each day. This can help promote a positive attitude and consciously recognize the blessings in your life.

Evening reflection: Take time each evening to reflect on the day. Ask yourself where you saw God at work in your life and how you responded to challenges. This reflection can help you grow spiritually and develop a deeper connection with God.

Through the regular practice of prayer and meditation, devotion and reflection, faith becomes a vibrant and integral part of daily life. These routines strengthen the connection with God and promote a life of trust and confidence.

4.3 Faith and Family

Faith-Based Education

Knowledge of religious and philosophical issues is central to faith-based education. Only through knowledge can we form accurate opinions and live our faith in a well-founded way. It is essential that children and young people know and understand the content of the faith in question. This knowledge is the basis for them to make a conscious and willing decision to live with God.

The importance of knowledge and understanding:

Religious Education: Children should not only learn about religious practices, but also develop a broad understanding of religious and philosophical issues. This will enable them to form their own opinions and recognize the importance of faith in their lives.

Content of Faith: It is important for children to know the basic tenets of the faith, such as the teachings of Jesus, the sacraments, and Christian values. This can be taught through regular Bible study, religious books, and conversations about faith.

Philosophical Questions: In addition to religious education, children and youth should be exposed to philosophical issues. This encourages critical thinking and helps them put their faith into a broader context.

Principles of religious education:

Role modeling: Parents should be role models and live their faith authentically. Children learn by observation and imitation. If they see their parents praying regularly, attending church, and living according to Christian values, they are more likely to adopt these behaviors.

Regular prayers and devotions: Incorporate daily prayers and devotions into the family routine. Shared morning, grace, and evening prayers can be a regular part of the daily routine. For example, the Lord's Prayer can be said together in the morning, the grace "Come, Lord Jesus" before meals, and the rosary in the evening.

Bible stories and teachings: Regularly read from the Bible and tell Bible stories that teach moral lessons. Children's Bibles with age-appropriate illustrations and stories can be very helpful.

Religious education: Attend church services and re-ligious education classes with your children. Sunday schools and church youth groups are great oppor-tunities to deepen faith and experience fellowship.

Shared religious rituals

Shared religious rituals strengthen family ties and and promote a community life of faith. They pro-vide opportunities for spiritual reflection and a shared experience of faith.

Examples of shared religious rituals and traditions include

Sunday worship: Regular attendance at Sunday worship is a central practice that spiritually strengthens the family and promotes fellowship with other believers.

Celebrating religious holidays: Christmas, Easter, Pentecost, and other Christian holidays provide special opportunities to celebrate the faith. Traditions such as setting up a nativity scene at Christmas or sharing breakfast at Easter can enrich these celebrations.

Marian devotion: May, as the month of Mary, is a good time to share Marian devotions. Praying the rosary or singing Marian hymns can be an integral part of family life.

Home blessings and pilgrimages: Regular house blessings by a priest and pilgrimages to holy places can enrich the religious life of the family.

Conflict Resolution

Faith can be a valuable resource in resolving family conflicts. Principles such as forgiveness, charity, and patience promote harmony and peace in the family.

How faith can help resolve family conflicts

Forgiveness: Christian teachings stress the importance of forgiveness. In family conflicts, a willingness to forgive can help heal hurts and strengthen relationships. Praying for God's help in forgiveness can be a first step.

Love of neighbor: Faith encourages charity, which manifests itself in understanding, compassion, and consideration. This can help ease tensions and resolve conflicts.

Prayer together: Praying together in conflict situations can bring peace and clarity. It allows people to focus on God and seek His guidance.

Spiritual counseling: Seeking spiritual counseling from a priest or pastor can help clarify conflicts and provide spiritual support.

4.4 Faith and Work

Ethics and morality in the workplace

Applying Christian principles in the workplace is an essential part of living out one's faith. Ethics and morality play a central role in this, providing guidance for daily actions in the workplace.

Applying Christian Principles:

Honesty and integrity: Christian ethics emphasize the importance of honesty and integrity in all aspects of life, including the workplace. This means always telling the truth, admitting mistakes, and dealing fairly with colleagues and customers.

Justice and Fairness: Justice and fairness are also important principles. This includes treating all employees fairly, paying them fairly and rejecting discrimination and injustice.

Responsibility and Reliability: Responsibility and dependability are essential virtues. A Christian should always strive to perform his or her duties reliably and conscientiously.

Charity and Compassion: The Christian teaching of charity can also be applied in professional life. This can be seen in compassion, helpfulness, and a willingness to help and support others.

Balancing work and faith

Integrating faith and work can be challenging, especially in a fast-paced and demanding work environment. However, it is possible to find a balance and integrate faith into your daily work life.

Strategies for balancing faith and work

Make time for prayer and meditation: Set aside time for prayer and meditation to strengthen your spiritual life. This can be done before work, during lunch, or after work.

Set priorities: Set clear priorities to balance work and personal life. Faith should be a regular part of your daily routine.

Faith symbols and rituals: Small reminders of your faith, such as a cross, a picture of a saint, or a Bible at work, can be a constant reminder of your spiritual values. Rituals such as saying a short prayer before making important decisions can help integrate faith into your daily work routine.

Stress management: Use your faith as a resource for coping with stress. Prayer, meditation, and trust in God's guidance can help you face professional challenges more calmly.

Witnessing in the workplace

Living and sharing your faith at work can be done through small gestures and by modeling Christian values. It is not about imposing your faith on others, but about being an authentic example.

How to live and share your faith at work:

Be a role model: Live your faith through your behavior. Honesty, fairness, and compassion will be noticed and appreciated by others.

Demonstrate openness: Be open about your faith when it comes naturally. Talk about your values and beliefs when appropriate topics come up.

Offer support: Offer support and help when colleagues need it. This can be in the form of practical assistance or prayer.

Seek community: Seek out like-minded people at work to share faith practices and strengthen each other. This can be done through prayer groups or informal gatherings.

Respect and tolerance: Show respect and tolerance for the beliefs and faiths of your co-workers.

Respectful interaction creates a positive work environment and encourages sharing.

4.5 Faith and Community

Participation in the community

Participation in community events and worship is an important expression of faith and plays a central role in the life of a Christian. This participation is not only for personal spiritual strengthening, but also for the building up of the community and the glory of God.

The Role of Participation in Church Events and Worship Services

Worship as a Testimony to the Glory of God: Church services, especially Holy Mass, are central events for the glory of God. They provide an opportunity to consciously acknowledge God, to appreciate His greatness and power, and to give Him glory. Participation in these services is an expression of our respect and devotion to God.

Holy Mass and the Sacrifice of Jesus Christ: In the Catholic Mass there is also the blessed repetition of the sacrifice of Jesus Christ for the redemption of mankind. Here, the Holy Mass is celebrated not only as a remembrance of the Last Supper with Jesus Christ, but it renews the divine grace of redemption and enables the faithful to participate sacramentally in this central mystery of faith. It is also a time for reflection, prayer, and spiritual renewal.

Building Community: Church events foster community and provide opportunities to share and support one another with other believers. These events can range from Bible study groups to prayer circles to social activities.

Social projects and missions

Christian faith is also expressed in our commitment to social projects and missionary work. These activities are an expression of charity and a mission to help others and spread the gospel.

Examples and suggestions for community-based social and mission projects include

Soup kitchens and food pantries: Many churches organize soup kitchens or food banks to help the needy in the community. These projects provide not only food, but also human warmth and support.

Children and youth programs: Congregations can offer programs to support children and youth, such as tutoring, recreational activities, and spiritual education. These programs promote not only personal development, but also faith.

Missions: Church members can participate in mission trips to bring the gospel to other parts of the world while providing practical help, such as building schools, providing medical care, and supporting local communities.

Environmental projects: Some churches are involved in environmental projects, such as planting community gardens or organizing litter cleanups. These projects promote awareness of creation and our responsibility to care for it.

Support and assistance

Faith can be a powerful motivation to help others in the community. Inspired by faith, we can actively contribute to improving the lives of others and strengthening the community.

How faith can help others in the community:

Practical help: Help neighbors and community members with everyday tasks such as shopping, yard work, or transportation to medical appointments. Small gestures of support can make a big difference.

Pastoral care and support: Offer pastoral support by listening to, praying for, and being with people in crisis. A listening ear and a comforting word can go a long way.

Educational opportunities: Get involved in educational opportunities, such as language classes for migrants or tutoring for schoolchildren. Education is a key to self-sufficiency and social participation.

Community outreach: Organize or participate in community-building activities such as community festivals, outings, or sporting events. Such activities build cohesion and a sense of community.

4.6 Conclusion of the Chapter

Summarize the main points:

In this chapter, we have explored the different ways in which faith can be put into practice in everyday life. We have emphasized the importance of personal spiritual practices, such as prayer and meditation, and given concrete examples and guidance on how to integrate them into daily life.

Personal Spiritual Practices: We discussed the central role of prayer and meditation, introduced various prayers, and gave practical tips on how to integrate these practices into everyday life. The importance of gratitude and self-reflection was also emphasized.

Faith and Family: The role of faith-based parenting, the principles and practices that support it, and how shared religious rituals can strengthen family bonds were explained. The role of faith in resolving family conflicts was also discussed.

Faith and work: We discussed how Christian principles can be applied in the workplace, how to balance work and faith, and how to live and share one's faith in the workplace.

Faith and community: The importance of participating in church events and worship was emphasized, as well as involvement in social projects and missionary work. We showed how faith can serve as a motivation to help others in the community.

Moving on to the next chapter:

In the next chapter, we will look at more in-depth topics and practical guidance on how to anchor and live out faith even more deeply in everyday life. We will explore how faith can be further strengthened and integrated into different areas of life, and we will offer concrete strategies and resources for achieving these goals.

Chapter 5:
Challenges in the Life of Faith

5.1 Introduction

Aim and purpose of the chapter

This chapter deals with the challenges that may arise in the life of faith. It is important to face these challenges because they are an essential part of the spiritual growth process. Doubts and crises are natural stages that every believer can go through. Dealing with these challenges not only strengthens faith, but also deepens understanding and relationship with God.

Doubts and crises are often times of change and reorientation. They provide opportunities to challenge, strengthen, and redefine one's faith. This chapter is designed to help readers prepare for such times and to give them tools to maintain and strengthen their faith in difficult times. At the same time, we want to show how faith can be lived out in a secular society, and what strategies can help to remain steadfast in the face of challenges and discrimination.

Overview of upcoming content

In the following sections of this chapter, we will cover various topics and challenges in the life of faith:

Dealing with doubts of faith: We will share strategies and practical approaches for dealing with doubts of faith. We will also share stories of people who have walked through their doubts and strengthened their faith as a result.

Times of crisis: We will explore how faith can provide support in times of personal or collective crisis. Examples from the lives of believers who have found their faith to be a support in such times will deepen these themes.

Faith in a Secular Society: In an often secular and atheistic environment, it is a challenge to live out one's faith openly. We will discuss strategies and tips for living your faith authentically and steadfastly.

Conflict and Persecution: Religious discrimination and persecution are real in many parts of the world. We will share stories and strategies for dealing with these challenges while remaining steadfast in your faith.

Practical ways to strengthen your faith: Finally, we will discuss practical approaches to strengthening faith, including the importance of community support, deepening spiritual practice, and the role of religious education.

This comprehensive presentation will help readers prepare for the challenges of the faith life and show them ways to overcome and grow from them.

5.2 Doubts and Crises

Dealing with doubts

Doubts of faith are a natural and often unavoidable experience in the spiritual life. They can arise for a variety of reasons, whether from personal challenges, intellectual questions, or social influences. Dealing with these doubts is crucial for spiritual growth and strengthening of faith.

Strategies for Dealing with Doubt

Acknowledge doubts: The first step in dealing with doubt in faith is to acknowledge its existence. It is important to recognize that doubt is normal and part of the spiritual growth process. Doubt can lead us to question and deepen our faith.

Seek knowledge: Education and knowledge are essential tools in dealing with doubts of faith. The study of Scripture, theological works, and philosophical texts can help to overcome intellectual doubts. Interaction with clergy and other believers can provide additional perspectives.

Prayer and meditation: Prayer and meditation are powerful ways to find inner peace and spiritual clarity. In prayer, we can ask God for guidance and understanding. Meditation can help calm the mind and focus on spiritual connection.

Fellowship and support: Sharing with other believers can provide great comfort and support. Fellowships and prayer groups are places where you can talk openly about doubts and seek solutions together.

Reflection and journaling: Keeping a spiritual journal can help you organize your thoughts and doubts. Reflecting on personal experiences and writing down insights can bring clarity and perspective.

Stories of Believers

- C.S. Lewis, a distinguished Christian writer and theologian, experienced intense doubts about faith in his youth. Lewis was an avowed atheist before turning to Christianity after a long intellectual and spiritual struggle. In his book Surprised by Joy, he describes his journey from atheism to faith and how intellectual searching and personal experience led him to embrace the Christian faith.

- Mother Teresa, known for her devotion to the poor and needy, also went through deep spiritual crises and doubts. In her private letters, published posthumously, she reveals that she went through long periods of darkness and doubt about God's presence. Despite these inner struggles, she held on to her faith and continued her work, inspired by the example of Jesus and her calling to serve those in need.

- John Henry Newman, a prominent theologian and convert to Catholicism, experienced intense doubts and struggles during his spiritual journey. His search for truth led him from the Anglican Church to the Catholic Church, eventually becoming one of the most influential theologians of the 19th century. In his writings, he shares his spiritual struggles and the deep convictions that eventually led him to Catholicism.

- Anne Lamott, an American author known for her honest and humorous memoirs, uses her books to describe her own spiritual journey and struggles with doubts about faith. Her candid and often humorous accounts offer a realistic look at the challenges and joys that faith can bring. Her works, such as "Traveling Mercies," show how she worked through doubt to find a deeper understanding and a stronger relationship with God.

These stories illustrate that doubt is a natural part of the life of faith, and that it can often be the starting point for deeper spiritual insight and a stronger relationship with God. Dealing with doubt requires courage, patience, and a willingness to embark on a spiritual journey.

Times of crisis

Faith is often tested in times of crisis. Personal or collective crises such as illness, loss, natural disasters or social upheaval can create profound challenges. However, faith can be an important source of comfort, strength and hope.

Faith in personal crises

Personal crises, such as illness, the loss of a loved one, or professional difficulties, can put faith to the test. At such times, faith can be a source of confidence and inner strength.

Illness and healing:

- Austrian neurologist and psychiatrist Viktor Frankl survived the concentration camp and found comfort and meaning in suffering through his faith and philosophy of "saying yes to life in spite of everything. His experiences and faith helped him develop a new perspective on life and help others find the strength to overcome difficult situations.

- Joni Eareckson Tada, a well-known author and speaker, was paralyzed in a diving accident. Despite this severe personal crisis, she found new meaning in life through her faith in God and founded Joni and Friends, an organization that supports people with disabilities.

Loss and grief:

- After the death of his wife, C.S. Lewis wrote "On Grief," a deeply moving book that documents his struggles and his faith in times of loss. His faith helped him cope with the pain and find new hope.

- Psychiatrist Elisabeth Kübler-Ross, known for her work on death and dying, found comfort in her faith and a deep spiritual connection that carried her through her professional and personal challenges.

Career and financial difficulties:

- Financial advisor Dave Ramsey experienced a severe financial crisis before getting back on his feet through faith and the application of biblical financial principles. Today, he helps others live fulfilled lives through debt freedom and financial management.

Faith in collective crises

Social or global crises, such as natural disasters or political unrest, also present significant challenges. In such times, faith can be a source of collective hope and solidarity.

Natural disasters

- 2010 Haiti earthquake: After the devastating earthquake in Haiti in 2010, churches and faith-based organizations played a central role in providing aid and support. Faith helped many people find hope and strength to survive the disaster.

- 2004 tsunami: After the 2004 Indian Ocean tsunami, many faith-based organizations and churches offered support and assistance. Faith gave many people strength and hope to cope with their losses.

Economic depression

- Great Depression of 1929: During the Great Depression, many people found comfort and support in their religious communities. Churches organized soup kitchens and relief projects to ease people's suffering. Faith helped many keep hope alive and support each other.

These examples show that faith can play an important role in times of personal and collective crisis, offering comfort, strength and hope. Through prayer, fellowship and the support of brothers and sisters in faith, believers can strengthen their faith and gain new perspectives in difficult times.

5.3 Social Challenges

Believing in a secular society

Living in a predominantly secular or atheist society can be challenging for people of faith. Culture and social norms can often be at odds with the values and beliefs of faith. It is important to develop strategies for living out your faith in an authentic and consistent way.

Living in a secular environment: Strategies for living out one's faith in a predominantly secular or atheist environment.

- Education and Knowledge: A solid knowledge of one's own beliefs and theological arguments is crucial. This not only helps to strengthen one's own faith, but also allows for respectful and informed discussion with those who think differently. Reading and studying the Bible and other religious scriptures, as well as the works of theologians and philosophers, can help deepen and intellectually support faith.

- Fellowship and support: Interacting with other believers in faith communities provides not only support, but also a platform for living out and sharing common values. Participation in Bible study groups, prayer groups, and other religious events builds a sense of community and provides valuable support in a secular environment.

- Active involvement: Participating in social and charitable projects demonstrates faith in action.

Not only can it help you live your faith authentically, but it can also set a positive example for others. By participating in community or religious organizations, you can have a positive impact on society and demonstrate how faith can enrich lives.

- Prayer and meditation: Regular prayer and meditation can help you focus on what is important and find inner peace and clarity. This is especially important in an environment that can often be distracting and challenging.

Authenticity and steadfastness: Tips on how to remain authentic and not hide your faith.

- Confidence and conviction: It is important to have confidence and conviction in your faith. This requires courage and inner strength to stand firm in an often critical environment. Developing a strong spiritual foundation through education, prayer, and reflection can help find this inner strength.

- Openness and dialogue: Open and respectful conversations about faith can help clarify misunderstandings and reduce prejudice. It is important to be prepared to answer questions and explain one's beliefs. Through dialogue, bridges can be built that lead to greater understanding and mutual appreciation.

- Integrity and consistency: Authenticity means living out one's faith in all areas of life, not just in private or church contexts. This requires integrity and consistency in behavior and choices. Living according to one's faith can be a powerful witness and example to others.

- Patience and tolerance: It is important to be patient and tolerant of those who think differently. Not everyone will understand or respect your beliefs, but with patience and tolerance, you can be a positive influence. Dealing respectfully with criticism and rejection shows strength and promotes peaceful coexistence.

These strategies help believers live their faith authentically and steadfastly in a secular society. They offer practical approaches to strengthening faith and demonstrate that religious beliefs can be a positive force in life and society.

Conflict and persecution

Faith and religion can often lead to conflict and discrimination in a secular or religiously critical society. It is important to develop strategies for dealing with these challenges and to be inspired by the stories of those who have persevered in the face of persecution.

Addressing religious discrimination

Religious discrimination can take many forms, from social exclusion to professional disadvantage to direct attacks. Dealing with this type of discrimination requires courage, wisdom and deep faith.

- Awareness and education: Educate yourself and others about your rights and the laws that protect religious freedom. This will help you defend yourself with confidence in situations of discrimination.

- Education and Dialogue: Encourage dialogue and education in your community to reduce prejudice and misunderstanding. Discrimination often stems from ignorance and fear of the unknown.

- Support and fellowship: Seek support from religious communities, organizations, and legal services that offer assistance in cases of discrimination. The support of a community can provide significant comfort and practical assistance.

- Networks and alliances: Network and form alliances with other faith communities and secular organizations that advocate for human rights and religious freedom.

- Inner strength and prayer: Prayer and meditation: Draw strength from prayer and meditation to stay strong and centered. These spiritual practices can help you find peace and clarity during difficult times.

- Examples and Inspiration: Be inspired by stories of how other believers have dealt with discrimination and remained strong.

Stories of Believers

- German theologian Dietrich Bonhoeffer, a prominent opponent of National Socialism, was imprisoned and eventually executed for his opposition to Hitler and his policies. Despite this extreme persecution, Bonhoeffer remained steadfast in his faith and found comfort and strength in his imprisonment through prayer and the writing of spiritual texts.

- Two Iranian Christians, Maryam Rostampour and Marziyeh Amirizadeh, were imprisoned for their faith and missionary activities. Despite the harsh conditions in prison, they held on to their faith and used their time to share their religion with other prisoners and to pray. Their story shows the courage and steadfastness that faith can give in difficult times.

Persecution: Examples of People Who Have Remained Steadfast in Their Faith Despite Persecution

Religious persecution is an unfortunate reality in many parts of the world. But even in the darkest of times, there are stories of strength of faith and unwavering conviction.

- Martin Luther King, Jr, a leading civil rights activist and Baptist preacher, fought tirelessly for equality and social justice despite repeated threats, arrests and eventual assassination. His faith in God and the biblical principles of justice and love carried him through many challenges and inspired his speeches and actions.

- Archbishop Oscar Romero of El Salvador spoke out against the violence and oppression of the military government and advocated for the poor and oppressed. Despite threats and eventual assassin-nation during a mass, he remained true to his faith and convictions.

- Asia Bibi, a Pakistani Christian, was sentenced to death for blasphemy and spent nearly a decade in prison before being acquitted. Despite the extreme hardships she endured, she remained true to her faith, finding comfort and strength in her prayer and conviction.

These stories show that faith can provide support even in the most difficult and dangerous situations. They are examples of the courage and steadfastness that faith can provide and offer inspiration to anyone facing challenges in their own faith life.

5.4 Practical Approaches to Strengthening Faith

Community support

The support of faith communities plays a crucial role in strengthening and consolidating faith. In a church, believers find not only spiritual support, but also social bonds and practical help.

- The Importance of Community: Community as Support: A faith community provides a network of people who share similar beliefs and values. This community can provide support in times of joy and sorrow, and helps to strengthen faith.

- Social Bonds: Participating in community activities fosters social bonds and creates a sense of belonging. This can be especially important if you live in an environment that does not share or support your faith.

- Practical help and support: Community projects: Many faith communities organize projects and events that provide practical help, such as soup kitchens, homeless shelters, and other charitable activities. These projects not only help those in need, but also provide an opportunity for members to live out their faith through action.

- Pastoral care and counseling: Many churches offer pastoral care and counseling, which can help with personal crises and doubts about faith. This support can be a valuable resource for strengthening faith and overcoming challenges.

Spiritual Practice

Deepening spiritual practice is an important part of strengthening faith. Regular prayer, meditation, and attendance at religious services are important elements of this practice.

- Prayer and Meditation: Pray regularly: Daily prayer is an essential practice for maintaining a close relationship with God. It provides an opportunity to express gratitude, ask for guidance, and find inner peace. Traditional prayers such as the Our Father and Hail Mary can be incorporated into the daily routine.
- Meditation: Meditation helps to quiet the mind and focus on God's presence. This practice can help achieve spiritual clarity and deepen faith.

- Attendance at religious services: Regular church services: Attending worship services is a way to celebrate and experience faith within a community. Worship services provide a structured opportunity for worship and reflection on spiritual issues.

- Sacraments and Rituals: Participating in sacraments and religious rituals, such as the Eucharist in Christianity, strengthens one's connection to God and the faith community.

Education and Knowledge

Religious education and knowledge of one's faith are essential to strengthening and deepening faith. A solid understanding of one's religion helps to defend one's faith and to overcome intellectual doubts.

- Study the scriptures: Study of the scriptures: Regular study of the Bible or other scriptures provides deep insight into the teachings and stories of the faith. Bible and study groups can help deepen understanding and strengthen faith.

- Theological works: Reading and studying theological works and the writings of church fathers, theologians, and spiritual teachers can help develop a deeper understanding of the faith.

Religious Education:

- Religious schools and educational institutions: Attending religious schools and educational institutions provides a well-rounded education in religious and theological subjects. This education helps to intellectually support and strengthen the faith.

- Online Courses and Seminars: Many religious organizations offer online courses and seminars that provide a flexible way to deepen religious education and interact with other believers.

These practical faith-building approaches offer ways to strengthen and deepen faith in everyday life. Community support, spiritual practice, and religious education are essential elements in developing a deep and abiding relationship with God and living faith in a secular world.

5.5 Conclusion of the Chapter

Summary of Key Points

In this chapter we have looked at the challenges believers face in their lives of faith, especially in an increasingly secular society. We have covered the following key points:

Doubts and crises

Strategies for dealing with doubts: education and knowledge, fellowship and support, prayer and meditation.

Stories of believers such as C.S. Lewis, Mother Teresa, John Henry Newman, and Anne Lamott who have experienced doubts and strengthened their faith.

In personal crises, faith offers comfort and strength, as the examples of Viktor Frankl and Joni Eareckson Tada demonstrate. In collective crises, such as natural disasters or economic depressions, faith plays an important role in providing support and community cohesion.

Social challenges

Living in a secular environment: Strategies for overcoming challenges to living faith authentically and steadfastly.

Authenticity and steadfastness: Tips for maintaining integrity and consistency in faith life.

Coping with religious discrimination: education and outreach, community and networking support, and inner strength through prayer and meditation.

Stories of steadfast believers such as Dietrich Bonhoeffer, Maryam Rostampour and Marziyeh Amirizadeh, and Asia Bibi, who maintained their faith in the face of persecution.

Practical approaches to strengthening faith:

Community Support: The importance of faith communities and their support.

Deepening spiritual practice through regular prayer, meditation, and participation in religious services.

Religious Education and Literacy: The role of religious education and knowledge in strengthening faith.

Transition to the next chapter

In the next chapter, we will look at more topics and practical ways to integrate faith more deeply into everyday life. We will provide concrete examples and tips on how faith can be actively lived and integrated into various areas of life.

Chapter 6:
Additional Topics and Practical Guidance

6.1 Introduction

Purpose and Aim of the Chapter

After the intensive examination of the basic principles and challenges of the life of faith in the previous chapters, this chapter aims to provide further topics and practical guidance. The purpose of this chapter is to provide readers with in-depth approaches and concrete steps for living and developing their faith in everyday life.

A life of faith requires constant learning and growth. It is not just about maintaining faith, but actively deepening and broadening it. This chapter aims to help readers keep their faith alive and relevant through advanced spiritual practices, intentional use of technology, interfaith dialogue, and practical guidance on lifestyle and community involvement.

Overview of upcoming content

This chapter covers a variety of topics that can enrich and strengthen faith in everyday life:

Advanced spiritual practices

Pilgrimages and spiritual retreats: The importance and benefits of spiritual journeys and retreats, as well as examples and testimonies of people who have incorporated these practices into their lives.

Rituals and Sacraments: An in-depth look at the importance of rituals and sacraments and practical guidance on how to incorporate them into daily life.

Faith in the Modern World

Technology and Faith: How technology can be used to deepen faith and advice on how to use digital media in an intentional and mindful way.

Interfaith Dialogue and Tolerance: The importance of dialogue with other faiths and practical tips for respectful and fruitful conversations.

Practical Lifestyle Guidance

Time Management and Priorities: Strategies for balancing faith and everyday life and tips for keeping faith at the center of your life.

Sustainability and Ethics: Guidance for living a sustainable, faith-centered lifestyle and practical ethical choices in everyday life.

Community and Social Action

Active community participation: The importance of community and examples of community involvement.

Social justice and mission: The role of faith in promoting social justice and practical guidance for engaging in social projects and missions.

Summary of key points

This chapter provides a wealth of additional topics and practical guidance for deepening and living out your faith in everyday life. It introduces various spiritual practices, shows the conscious use of technology and the importance of interfaith dialogue, offers practical guidance on lifestyle, and emphasizes the importance of community and social involvement.

6.2 Continuing Spiritual Practices

Pilgrimages and spiritual retreats

Importance and benefits

Pilgrimages and spiritual retreats are powerful ways to deepen faith and find a deeper connection with God. They provide a welcome break from the hustle and bustle of everyday life and allow for an intensive examination of one's faith and spiritual questions.

Pilgrimages

Significance: Pilgrimages have a long tradition in many religions. They symbolize the search for spiritual renewal and the quest for a deeper connection with God. Walking in the footsteps of holy sites can deepen faith and open new perspectives.

Benefits: Pilgrimages offer an opportunity to step away from daily distractions and focus on the spiritual experience. They encourage self-reflection and can have a transformative effect on one's life of faith.

Spiritual Retreats

Significance: A spiritual retreat is a time of reflection and prayer, often in a monastery or other secluded place. These times of silence and prayer provide an opportunity to deepen one's faith and gain new spiritual insights.

Benefits: Retreats provide an opportunity to get away from the hustle and bustle of everyday life and focus on one's faith. They promote inner peace and can help build a deeper relationship with God.

Examples and Testimonies

Pilgrimages

- Camino de Santiago: One of the most famous pilgrimages is the Camino de Santiago, which leads to Santiago de Compostela in Spain. Many pilgrims report deep spiritual experiences and a strengthening of their faith through this journey. One example is Hape Kerkeling, a well-known German entertainer, who describes his experiences on the Camino de Santiago in his book 'Ich bin dann mal weg'. He speaks of a deep inner transformation and a new perspective on his life and faith.

- Fatima, in Portugal, is a major pilgrimage site where the Virgin Mary appeared to three shepherd children in 1917. Pilgrims travel to Fatima from all over the world to pray at the holy sites associated with the Marian apparitions. Particularly impressive are the candlelight processions that take place each year on May 13 and October 13, in which thousands of faithful participate. Many pilgrims report deep spiritual experiences and inner peace found at Fatima.

- Lourdes, in the south of France, is one of the most famous pilgrimage sites in the world. It was here that the Virgin Mary appeared to a young girl named Bernadette Soubirous in 1858. The Grotto of Massabielle, where the apparitions took place, attracts millions of pilgrims who come to drink water from the springs, which are believed to have healing properties. Many people, including the terminally ill, travel to Lourdes in the hope of healing or to find solace and spiritual renewal.

- Rome, the Eternal City, is the center of the Catholic Church and an important place of pilgrimage. Pilgrims visit the four major basilicas, especially St. Peter's Basilica, built on the tomb of the Apostle Peter. The city offers numerous spiritual sites and relics that attract devout Christians from all over the world. The experience of visiting the holy sites of early Christianity and the heart of the Catholic Church deepens the faith of many pilgrims.

- Loretto, Italy, is famous for the "Holy House," which, according to legend, was the home of the Virgin Mary in Nazareth and was brought to Loretto by angels. For centuries, the place has been a destination for pilgrims seeking to get closer to the faith and to the Virgin Mary. Loretto is known for its tranquility and the opportunity to reflect and deepen one's faith.

- Medjugorje, in Bosnia-Herzegovina, is a modern pilgrimage site known for reports of Marian apparitions since 1981. Although the apparitions are not yet officially recognized by the Catholic Church, the place attracts millions of pilgrims each year. Many report deep spiritual experiences and renewed faith. Medjugorje is also known for the many confessions and conversions that take place there.

- The Holy Land: A pilgrimage to the Holy Land, especially to Jerusalem, Bethlehem and Nazareth, enables believers to visit the places where Jesus Christ lived, preached, died and rose again. This pilgrimage is considered particularly significant because it brings the biblical stories to life and provides a deep connection to the history of the Christian faith. Pilgrims often report a greater understanding of their faith and a deeper relationship with God after visiting these holy sites.

Specialized travel agencies offer many pilgrimages to holy sites in Europe and around the world. These trips are often well organized and offer participants the opportunity to deepen their faith in community with other pilgrims.

Spiritual Retreats

- The Maria Engelport Monastery in the Flaumbach Valley near the Mosel River regularly offers retreats and spiritual exercises that allow participants to explore their faith and find a deeper spiritual connection with God.

- Marienrode Monastery near Hildesheim also offers retreats and spiritual exercises. These times of reflection and prayer help participants find inner peace and deepen their faith.

- The Benedictine Monastery of Andechs on the Holy Mountain in Bavaria offers spiritual retreats and days of reflection in addition to its famous pilgrimage church. The combination of awe-inspiring nature and spiritual retreat makes this place especially attractive to people seeking a deeper connection to their faith.

- Ottobeuren Abbey (Bavaria). This Benedictine monastery in the Allgäu region offers a variety of spiritual programs, including retreats and days of silence. The beautiful Baroque architecture and spiritual atmosphere make Ottobeuren an ideal place for retreats and reflection.

- The Benedictine Abbey of Maria Laach on Lake Laach is known not only for its breathtaking Romanesque architecture, but also for its year-round spiritual programs. Retreats and meditation days help visitors develop a deeper relationship with God.

- Ettal Monastery (Bavaria). Located in the foothills of the Bavarian Alps, the Benedictine Monastery of Ettal offers retreats and spiritual seminars that focus on deepening personal faith and inner renewal.

- Heiligenkreuz Monastery (Austria). This Cistercian monastery near Vienna is one of the oldest and most important monasteries in Central Europe. It offers regular retreats and spiritual exercises that allow participants to get away from the stresses of everyday life and deepen their spiritual practice.

- Santuario di San Francesco del Deserto (Italy). This Franciscan monastery on a small island in the Venetian lagoon offers a particularly peaceful and secluded environment for spiritual retreats. It is known for its silence and reflection on the simplicity and teachings of St. Francis of Assisi.

- Eberbach Monastery (Hesse). Nestled among the vineyards of the Rheingau region, this former Cistercian monastery offers an impressive setting for spiritual retreats. The serene atmosphere of the monastery encourages peace and reflection, helping visitors to deepen their faith and draw new strength.

These places offer a wide variety of opportunities for spiritual retreats. Each location has its own special atmosphere and history, which can make the spiritual retreat a unique experience.

Retreats and Religious Education Programs:

Retreats: Retreats are spiritual exercises often offered by church groups and communities. They provide a structured opportunity to deepen faith and have spiritual experiences. Examples include the Jesuit retreat house in Münster or the Benedictine monastery in Nütschau near Hamburg, which regularly offers programs for various target groups.

Religious education programs: Many religious communities offer programs for religious education and spiritual renewal. These programs help participants develop a deeper understanding of their faith and strengthen their spiritual practice.

These examples show how pilgrimages and spiritual retreats can help deepen faith and find a stronger connection with God. They provide a valuable opportunity to get away from the distractions of everyday life and focus on the spiritual experience.

Rituals and Sacraments

Deepening Understanding

Holy Mass:

The Holy Mass, especially in Catholic Christianity, is of central importance. It is more than a worship service; it is the liturgical celebration of Christ's sacrifice on the cross. The Catholic Church teaches that the Mass is the sacramental renewal of the Sacrifice of the Cross through which the salvation of humanity continues.

Renewal of the Sacrifice of the Cross: In every Mass, the sacrifice of Christ on the Cross is made present. It is not a repetition, but a sacramental re-presentation. Christ, the High Priest, offers himself to the Father as a sacrifice for the sins of mankind.

Communion and Eucharist: The faithful attend Mass to celebrate communion with Christ and with one another. Through the Eucharist, they receive the Body and Blood of Christ, which strengthens their union with Him and with the Church.

The Seven Sacraments:

The Catholic Church recognizes seven sacraments, which are considered visible signs of God's invisible grace. Each sacrament has a special meaning and plays an essential role in the life of the believer.

Baptism

Significance: Baptism is the first sacrament and initiation into the Christian community. It cleanses

one from original sin and all personal sins and confers new life in Christ.

Ritual: Baptism is administered by immersion in water or by pouring water over the person, accompanied by the words: "I baptize you in the name of the
Father and of the Son and of the Holy Ghost."

Confirmation

Significance: Confirmation reinforces the grace of
baptism and confers the gift of the Holy Spirit. It enables believers to live as full members of the Church
and to profess their faith publicly.

Ritual: Confirmation is performed by the bishop or
an authorized priest through the laying on of hands
and anointing with chrism oil.

Eucharist (Communion)

Meaning: The Eucharist is the sacrament of the
presence of Christ in the form of bread and wine. It
is the central sacrament of the Christian community
and the sacrament of unity.

Ritual: During Holy Mass, bread and wine are
changed into the body and blood of Christ. The

faithful receive the Eucharist as nourishment for their souls and as a sign of communion with Christ and the Church.

Marriage

Meaning: Marriage is the sacrament of a lifelong union between a man and a woman. It symbolizes Christ's faithful and indissoluble love for His Church.

Ritual: Marriage is celebrated by a mutual promise of marriage before a priest and two witnesses. The couple confer the sacrament on each other by their free and conscious will to enter into marriage.

Priesthood (Ordination)

Meaning: Priestly ordination is the sacrament by which men are placed in the service of the Church to administer the sacraments and lead the congregation.

Ritual: Ordination is performed by the laying on of hands and the bishop's prayer. The ordained person receives the authority to administer the sacraments and lead the congregation.

Confession (Penance)

Significance: Confession is the sacrament of reconciliation through which sins committed after baptism are forgiven. It provides an opportunity for repentance and renewed union with God and the Church, provided the sins are sincerely confessed and sincerely repented of.

Ritual: The believer confesses his sins to a priest and receives forgiveness through the prayer of absolution. Forgiveness is granted by the priest acting in the person of Jesus Christ, as only God can forgive sins.

Anointing of the Sick (Extreme Unction)

Significance: The Anointing of the Sick is the sacrament that strengthens and heals the sick and dying. It brings comfort, peace, and forgiveness of sins.

Ritual: The Anointing of the Sick is performed by the laying on of hands and anointing with holy oil, accompanied by prayers for healing and strengthening.

Note: It is important to note that not all Christian churches recognize these seven sacraments. Some

Protestant churches recognize only baptism and the Eucharist as sacraments, while other Christian denominations have different views on the number and importance of the sacraments.

Practical guidance

Integration into daily life

Daily devotions: Use short prayers and meditations to keep the sacraments alive in daily life. Begin the day with a prayer that recalls baptism and end the day with an act of penance.

Attend Mass regularly: Attend Mass regularly to receive the Eucharist and strengthen your communion with Christ.

Family Rituals

Sacramental Preparation: Prepare yourself and your family for the sacraments by discussing the meaning and process of the sacraments and praying together.

Celebrating the sacraments: Celebrate the sacraments as special occasions in family life. Baptism,

First Communion, Confirmation, and marriage are milestones that enrich the life of faith.

Parish Life

Sacramental ministries: Get involved in your parish by participating in sacramental celebrations and helping others receive the sacraments.
Formation: Participate in classes and retreats that deepen your understanding and appreciation of the sacraments.

6.3 Faith in the Modern World

Technology and Faith

Use of Technology

In today's digital age, technology offers many opportunities to deepen faith and integrate spiritual practices into daily life. From various apps to online communities to digital resources, there are many tools that can help the faithful in their spiritual journey.

Apps

Prayer apps: There are numerous apps that offer daily prayers, Bible verses, and devotions. Examples include the Laudate and Bible App apps, which offer a variety of prayers and spiritual texts.

Meditation apps: Apps such as "Abide" offer Christian meditations and guided prayers that can help calm the mind and focus on God.

Radio Maria: Radio Maria offers an extensive program available digitally and online. Worship services, prayer circles, and spiritual talks are broadcast daily. Of particular note is the daily rosary, which listeners can actively participate in.

Online communities

Social media: Platforms such as Facebook, Instagram and X offer communities where believers can share ideas, prayer requests and spiritual support. Groups such as "Christians on Facebook" or "Communio Online" are examples of such communities.

Web sites and forums: Websites such as "Christianity.com" or "katholisch.de" offer forums and discussion groups where believers can ask questions, engage in discussions, and share their spiritual journeys.

Digital Resources

Online Bibles: Websites such as "bibel-online.net" offer online Bibles in various translations and languages, allowing believers to read Scripture anytime, anywhere.

E-Books and Podcasts: Many publishers offer religious e-books, and there are a variety of podcasts on spiritual topics. These resources can be listened to on the commute to work or during leisure time to strengthen the faith.

Streaming services: Many churches offer their services and events online for streaming. This is a wonderful way to gain insight into these ceremonies and to participate remotely.

Caution and mindfulness

While technology offers many benefits, it is important to use it consciously and mindfully to avoid distractions and keep the focus on faith.

Minimize distractions

Conscious use: Set clear boundaries for your use of technology. Use apps and digital resources specifically for your spiritual needs and avoid unnecessary distractions.

Reduce screen time: Limit the time you spend on non-spiritual activities to make more room for prayer, meditation, and reflection.

Focus on faith

Daily rituals: Incorporate regular times for prayer and meditation into your daily routine to ensure that your faith is central. Use technology to support these rituals, but do not let it dominate them.

Practice mindfulness: Practice mindfulness to stay present and find a deeper connection with God. Use meditation apps or guided prayers to enhance your mindfulness.

Cultivate community

Online and offline communities: Use digital platforms to stay in touch with other believers, but don't forget the importance of face-to-face meetings and local congregations. Attend worship services and community events regularly to maintain a balanced spiritual practice. It is important to emphasize that streaming services cannot replace physical presence in spiritual acts. The one exception is online prayer circles, especially with active listener participation. Otherwise, physical participation is always preferable to a digital forum.

Interfaith Dialogue and Tolerance

Importance of Dialogue

Interfaith dialogue is an essential component of peaceful and respectful coexistence in a pluralistic society. It promotes understanding and respect between people of different faiths and helps to avoid misunderstandings and prejudices. Here are some reasons why interfaith dialogue is important:

Promotes understanding

Reducing prejudice: Through dialogue, we learn about the beliefs and practices of other religions, which reduces prejudice and promotes a deeper understanding of one another.

Broadening our horizons: Interacting with people of other faiths enriches our own religious understanding and can open new perspectives on our own faith.

Promoting peace

Avoiding conflict: Through dialogue, potential conflicts can be identified early and avoided through understanding and cooperation.

Shared values: Many religions share basic ethical principles such as respect for human dignity, compassion and justice. These shared values can serve as a basis for cooperation and peaceful coexistence. Strengthening one's own faith practice

Reflection and deepening: Interreligious exchange challenges us to reflect and deepen our own faith. It can help us formulate our beliefs more clearly and live them more consciously.

Witnessing to faith: Dialogue provides an opportunity to witness to one's faith in a respectful way and to share it with others.

Practical Tips

In order to have respectful and fruitful conversations with people of other faiths, some principles and approaches are helpful:

Respect and openness

Active listening: Show genuine interest in the other person's beliefs and experiences. Listen actively without rushing to judgment or contradiction.

Respectful treatment: Treat the other person with respect and avoid condescending or derogatory comments. Respect the sacred texts, rituals, and symbols of the other religion.

Emphasize common ground

Shared values: Focus on the ethical and moral principles that many religions share, such as compassion, justice, and peace. These commonalities can provide a basis for dialogue.

Shared goals: Look for common goals, such as promoting peace, social justice and environmental protection, that transcend religious differences.

Clarity and honesty

Be clear about your own beliefs: Be honest and clear about your own beliefs. Avoid diluting or hiding your beliefs.

Ask questions: Ask open and respectful questions to learn more about your interviewer's beliefs and practices. This shows your interest and encourages deeper understanding.

Patience and willingness to learn

Be patient: Interfaith dialogue takes time and patience. Be prepared to build long-term relationships and to learn continuously.
Be willing to learn: Be open to new insights and willing to challenge and correct your own biases and misconceptions.

Events and forums

Interfaith forums: Participate in interfaith forums and events that promote interfaith exchange and understanding.

Community Projects: Get involved in community projects, such as social or environmental initiatives, that bring people of different faiths together.

Dealing with rejection and aggression

In an increasingly pluralistic and often tense world, Christians may encounter rejection or aggressive reactions. Here are some strategies for dealing with such situations:

Keep Calm

Maintain composure: Respond calmly to aggressive behavior. Do not be provoked, and remain polite and respectful.

Show understanding: Try to understand the reasons for the aggression. These reactions are often the result of misunderstandings or negative experiences.

Set boundaries

Communicate clearly: Set clear boundaries and communicate them calmly and clearly. Let the person know that disrespectful behavior is not acceptable.

Maintain safety: In extreme cases where safety is at risk, withdraw and seek assistance from a third party or authority.

Prayer and Support

Pray for the aggressors: Pray for those who attack or discriminate against you. Ask God for peace and understanding on both sides.

Community support: Seek support from your faith community. Share your experiences and ask for counsel and prayer.

Long-term solutions

Education and awareness: Engage in education and outreach to reduce misunderstanding and prejudice.

Promote dialogue: Engage in long-term interfaith dialogue to promote better understanding and peaceful coexistence.

6.4 Practical Lifestyle Guidelines

Time Management and Priorities

Balancing faith and daily life

Integrating faith into daily life requires conscious and structured time management. Here are some tips for organizing your day in a way that does not neglect your faith:

Establish daily routines

Begin the day with a short prayer or meditation. This can help you begin the day in a spiritual setting and connect with God.

Lunchtime prayer: Use your lunch hour for a brief prayer or reflection. This can help renew your focus on faith and give structure to your day.

Evening prayer: End the day with prayer, thanksgiving, and reflection. This is an opportunity to review the day and thank God for the blessings you have experienced.

Time for worship and fellowship

Weekly worship services: Schedule regular times to attend worship services. This will strengthen your connection to the church and deepen your faith.

Prayer groups and religious events: Attend prayer groups, Bible studies, or other religious events to fellowship with other believers and strengthen your own faith.

Use technology

Apps and online communities: Use religious apps that offer prayer schedules and Bible reading plans to integrate your faith into your daily life. Online communities can also help you stay connected in your faith.

Prioritize

To keep faith at the center of your life, it is important to set clear priorities. Here are some ways to do this:

Making faith a core priority

Make a conscious decision to make faith a central priority in your life.
This decision should be reflected in your daily actions and choices.
Life Planning: Integrate faith practices into your life plan. Include times for prayer, worship, and spiritual activities in your daily life.

Integrate faith into all areas of your life

Family and work: Integrate faith into your family life and work. This can be done by praying together, making ethical decisions at work, and being a role model.

Leisure and hobbies: Use your leisure time and hobbies to live out and deepen your faith. This can be done by reading religious literature, attending spiritual retreats, or volunteering in the community.

Ongoing reflection and adaptation

Regular review: Review your priorities regularly and adjust them as needed. Ask yourself if your life reflects your faith and if there are areas where you can integrate your faith more fully.

Spiritual guidance: Seek spiritual guidance and support from mentors, spiritual leaders, or the church to help you set and live your priorities clearly.

Further reflection

Balancing faith with everyday life and setting priorities requires constant attention and commitment. By making intentional choices and integrating faith practices into all areas of life, believers can keep their faith at the center of their lives. This leads to a more fulfilling and meaningful life that is in harmony with one's spiritual beliefs.

Stewardship of Creation

God expects us to be responsible and caring stewards of His creation. This treatment is an ethical and moral obligation deeply rooted in faith. Conscious and respectful stewardship of the environment and our fellow creatures is an expression of our faith and reverence for God's work.

Biblical Foundations

Creation mandate of stewardship: In Genesis 2:15, man is placed in the Garden of Eden to cultivate and care for it. This responsibility is still relevant today, calling us to protect and steward the natural world.

Care for creation: Psalm 24:1 reminds us that the earth and everything that lives on it belongs to the Lord. This implies an obligation not to destroy or abuse creation.

Practical approaches

Consume responsibly: Be mindful of moderate and conscious consumption of resources. This includes being mindful of food, clothing, and other necessities.

Protection of fellow creatures: Show respect and care for animals and plants. This can be done by supporting balanced agricultural practices and protecting habitats.

Community involvement: Participate in projects and initiatives that protect and care for the environment. This can be done through volunteer work or by supporting organizations dedicated to caring for creation.

Ethics in everyday life

Acting ethically in everyday life is a core aspect of living out one's faith. The guideline "Do to others as you would have them do to you" (Luke 6:31) and the certainty that we must justify our actions to God should guide our daily actions.

Ethical Principles

Golden Rule: The Golden Rule calls us to treat others with respect, justice, and love. This rule is universally applicable and forms the basis for ethical behavior in everyday life.

Divine Commandments: The Ten Commandments and the teachings of Jesus provide clear guidance for moral behavior. They help us live our lives according to the principles of love of neighbor and reverence for God.

Practical applications

Workplace: Act honestly and fairly in your work. Be fair to your co-workers and treat them with respect and dignity. Avoid dishonest practices and stand up for justice in the workplace.

Community and Family: Promote an atmosphere of love and respect in your family and community. Support the needs of those around you and work for social justice.

Consumer Behavior: Be an informed shopper and choose products that are ethically produced. Support businesses that promote fair labor conditions and environmentally sound practices.

Resources for Ethical Action

Church guidelines: Use your church's teachings and resources to support your ethical actions. Many churches offer programs and materials to help you make moral decisions.

Community support: Seek the counsel and support of your faith community to help you meet ethical challenges and work together for good.

In Conclusion

A responsible and ethical lifestyle is deeply rooted in faith. By treating creation with respect and acting ethically in our daily lives, we live out our connection to God and our fellow human beings in a way that is consistent with our faith. These principles help us live full and meaningful lives and have a positive impact on our environment and society.

6.5 Community and Social Involvement

Active participation in the community:

Importance of Community

Active participation in community activities is an essential part of the life of faith. Community is not only a source of support and inspiration, but also a place where faith is lived and strengthened. Here are some reasons why it is important to actively participate in ward activities:

Strengthen your faith

Worship together: Participating in worship services and religious ceremonies provides an opportunity to join with other believers in honoring God and celebrating faith. This can deepen and strengthen one's personal faith life.

Teaching and education: Community events often provide opportunities for faith education, whether through sermons, Bible studies, or religious workshops. These events help to deepen understanding and knowledge of the faith.

Support and Encouragement

Fellowship support: In a church, believers find support during difficult times. The church provides a network of people who can help and encourage in times of need.

Encouragement from role models: Meeting other believers who are actively living out their faith can be inspiring and encouraging. These role models show how faith can be put into practice in everyday life.

Promoting charity

Community efforts: By participating in community events, believers can initiate and carry out projects together to help those in need. This encourages charity and compassion.

Volunteerism: Many churches offer volunteer opportunities, whether it is helping with events, supporting social projects, or maintaining church facilities.

Examples of involvement

Here are some stories and tips for getting involved in your community:

Getting Involved in Church Administration

Example: Anna is a member of her parish council. She helps organize events, manages finances, and helps plan worship services. Through her work, she contributes to the structure and functioning of the church.

Tip: Ask your local ward about opportunities to help with administration or organization. All help is appreciated and contributes to the life of the church.

Leading Bible Groups

Example: Michael leads a weekly Bible group where believers read and discuss the Bible together. This group provides a space for sharing and deepening faith.

Tip: If you have a special interest in the Bible, consider leading or participating in a Bible study group. This fosters a sense of fellowship and learning together.

Service projects and initiatives

Example: St. Mark's regularly organizes soup kitchens for the homeless. Sarah and Thomas help prepare and serve the meals. Their involvement helps those in need and fosters a spirit of charity.

Tip: Look for community service projects in your area that you can get involved with. It could be anything from organizing a food pantry to visiting a nursing home.

Further Thoughts

Active participation in Church activities is an important part of the life of faith. It provides an opportunity for corporate worship, support and encouragement, and the promotion of charity.

Through community involvement, believers can live and strengthen their faith in everyday life.

Social Justice and Mission:

The role of faith

Faith plays a central role in promoting social justice. The principles of charity, mercy and justice, which are found in many religious teachings, motivate believers to work for a more just and humane society.

Biblical Foundations

Charity: In Mark 12:31, Jesus emphasizes that the second greatest commandment is to love your neighbor. This love of neighbor is the foundation for social justice work.

Compassion: In Luke 6:36, Jesus calls his followers to be compassionate as God is compassionate. This compassion is demonstrated in commitment to the weak and disadvantaged.

Practical applications

Help those in need: Believers are called to care for the poor, the sick, and the weak. This can be done through direct assistance, such as donating food or supporting service projects.

Promoting justice: A commitment to social justice includes fighting injustice and discrimination. This can be done through political advocacy, educational programs and awareness raising.

Community involvement

Community service: Many communities organize projects to help those in need, such as soup kitchens, clothing drives, or educational programs. These projects provide a platform for community involvement.

Mission and evangelism: Missionary activities that spread the faith while providing social support are another important aspect of community involvement.

Practical guidance

Here are some practical tips for getting involved in social and mission projects:

Find a project that matches your interests and skills: Think about the type of project that best matches your interests and skills. Whether it's working with the homeless, helping families in need, or teaching, there are many ways to get involved.

Community and Organizations: Check out the projects offered by your community or local religious organizations. There are often many ways to get involved.

Set realistic goals

Time and resources: Think about how much time and resources you can devote to your involvement. Set realistic goals to ensure sustainable and effective involvement.

Long-term commitment: Social justice and mission often require a sustained, long-term commitment. Think about how you can contribute on an ongoing and sustainable basis.

Work as a team

Strength in community: Social projects and missions are often more effective when done as a team. Work with others to achieve greater impact and support each other.

Leverage networks: Leverage existing networks and partnerships to support and expand your work. This can be done by collaborating with other communities, organizations or social institutions.

Education and training

Professional expertise: Social justice and mission often require specialized knowledge and skills. Participate in training and continuing education to enhance your expertise and make your work more effective.

Spiritual Strengthening: In addition to professional training, spiritual strengthening is important. Use spiritual exercises, prayer and reflection to strengthen your motivation and faith.

Conclusion

Faith motivates us to work for social justice and mission. By engaging in social projects and missionary activities, we can help make the world a more just and humane place. These activities strengthen not only the community, but also our own faith and spiritual connection.

6.6 Conclusion of the Chapter

Summary of Key Points

Throughout this chapter, we have explored various aspects of putting faith into practice. Here are the key takeaways:

Active Participation in the Church

Importance of community: We have emphasized the importance of active participation in community events and how these help to strengthen faith and promote charity.

Examples of involvement: We provided examples and practical tips on how to get involved in the church, whether through administrative work, leading Bible study groups, or participating in service projects.

Social Justice and Mission

The role of faith: Faith motivates us to promote social justice and to stand up for the weak and disadvantaged.

Practical guidance: We gave practical tips on how to get involved in social projects and missions, and emphasized the importance of community service.

Encouragement to Apply

As we conclude this chapter, we encourage you to apply the insights and examples to your own daily life. Here are a few practical tips:

Set realistic goals.

Start with small steps. Choose one or two or two areas in which you want to get involved, and set achievable goals.

Use your strengths and interests

Think about how you can use your skills and interests to serve your community and society. Your individual talents are valuable and can make a big difference.

Seek community

Connect with other community members and look for ways to work together. Community projects and shared spiritual practices strengthen not only faith but also a sense of community.

Stay consistent

Regularity is key to deepening your faith. Whether it's prayer, meditation, volunteering, or attending religious services, consistent practice will strengthen and deepen your faith.

Keep learning

Take advantage of the educational opportunities offered by your parish and other religious institutions. Continuing your education in the faith will help you deepen your knowledge and enrich your spiritual practice.

Conclusion

Practicing faith in everyday life is an ongoing process that requires patience, commitment, and consistency. By integrating the principles and practices presented in this chapter into your daily life, you can strengthen your faith while making a positive contribution to your community and society.

Chapter 7:
Conclusion and Outlook

7.1 Review of the Journey

Summary of Key Points

This book has taken you on a journey to explore and understand faith in a personal God as a conscious choice. Let's summarize the key themes and insights from each chapter:

Introduction and Purpose of the Book

Background and Motivation: We began with a detailed description of the current cultural and moral crisis in our society. The increasing relativization of values and norms, the disintegration of family structures, and the general crisis of meaning were highlighted.

The Need for a Transcendent Reference Point: It was argued that a return to a conscious belief in a personal God is the central solution for finding a way out of this crisis.

The possibility of a way out

The conscious act of will: We explained that belief in God can be a conscious, rational choice supported by philosophical and scientific arguments.

Transcendent values and standards: The importance of transcendent, absolute values and standards was explained, and how these can serve as moral guidelines.

Practical Examples and Inspiration

Testimonials and personal transformations: Stories of people who have experienced profound changes in their lives through faith were presented.

Principles and practices for daily life: Concrete examples and instructions were given on how to integrate and strengthen faith in daily life.

Practical application of faith in daily life

Personal spiritual practices: The importance of prayer, meditation, and daily devotions in strengthening personal faith was explained.

Faith and family: Principles of faith-based parenting, shared religious rituals, and conflict resolution within the family were presented.

Faith and Work: Discussed applying Christian principles in the workplace, balancing work and faith, and witnessing in the workplace.

Faith and community: The importance of participating in community events, social involvement and supporting others through faith were discussed.

Challenges in the life of faith

Doubts and Crises: Strategies for dealing with doubts and personal and collective crises were presented.

Social challenges: Dealing with a secular environment, religious discrimination and persecution were discussed.

Other topics and practical guidance

Spiritual practices: The importance of pilgrimages, spiritual retreats, rituals and sacraments were explained.

Faith in the modern world: The use of technology to deepen faith, interfaith dialogue and tolerance were discussed.

Lifestyle Practices: Tips on time management, prioritization, sustainability, and ethics.

Community and social engagement: Emphasized the importance of active community participation and commitment to social justice and mission.

Emphasizing Key Messages

The central message of this book is that belief in a personal God is a conscious, rational, and transformative choice that can positively impact both individual lives and communities. Transcendent values and standards provide a stable foundation for moral action and can offer guidance in an often chaotic and relativistic world. The active application of faith in everyday life, in the family, at work, and in the community is essential to strengthening and living faith.

By consciously choosing faith in God and actively integrating it into our lives, we can not only overcome personal crises, but also make a positive contribution to society and experience a deeper, more fulfilling existence.

7.2 Personal Reflection and Application

Encouragement for reflection

At the end of this journey, we encourage you to take time for personal reflection. The path of conscious faith is an ongoing journey that can bring both challenges and profound changes. Reflect on your personal journey and the changes you have experienced since beginning this book.

Self-reflection questions

What new insights about faith have you gained? Consider what new perspectives and insights you have gained from reading this book.

How has your view of God and faith changed? Think about whether and how your view of God and your faith have evolved.

And if you have already decided to believe in God:

What practical changes have you made in your life? Consider what concrete steps you have taken to integrate faith into your daily life.

What challenges have you faced and how have you overcome them? Think about the difficulties you encountered along the way and how you overcame them.

How have your relationships changed? Think about how your relationships with family, friends, and community have changed as a result of your intentional faith.

Application to Daily Life

In order to integrate the principles and practices discussed in this book into your daily life on a permanent basis, we would like to give you some specific tips and instructions:

Daily Spiritual Practice

Prayer and Meditation: Find a set time and quiet place for your daily prayer and meditation. This could be in the morning after you get up, during a lunch break, or in the evening before you go to bed.

Devotions and Bible Reading: Incorporate daily devotions and Bible reading into your daily routine. You can also use apps or online resources to support your spiritual practice.

Build commitment and regularity

Routines: Create regular routines for your spiritual practices. This will help you integrate these practices into your daily life.

Self-Discipline: Practice self-discipline to maintain your spiritual routines even during busy or difficult times.

Community and Support

Active Participation: Become actively involved in your community. Attend religious services and community events regularly to deepen your spiritual practice and find support.

Connect with like-minded people: Connect with other believers to share your experiences and support each other.

Education and training

Religious Education: Take advantage of religious education opportunities, whether through books, classes, or online resources. A deeper knowledge of the content of your faith will strengthen your convictions and help you better integrate them into your daily life.

Reflect and learn: Make regular time for reflection and learning. Consider what new aspects of your faith you would like to discover and how you can integrate them into your life.
Ethical Behavior

Ethical Decisions: Make conscious ethical decisions in your daily life. Consider whether each action is consistent with your faith principles.

Social Responsibility: Get involved in social projects and missions to live out your faith through practical action and make a positive contribution to society.

Concluding Reflections

Conscious faith is a lifelong journey that involves both personal and spiritual transformation. Through regular reflection and consistent application of the principles and practices presented in this book, you can deepen your faith and live a more fulfilling life. Be encouraged to continue on this path and enjoy the changes that conscious faith brings to your life.

7.3 Outlook and Inspiration

Future Challenges

Prepare for future challenges: The path of conscious faith is an ongoing journey that can be filled with challenges and trials. It is important to be prepared and to know that faith can be a strong support in overcoming these challenges. Future challenges can come in many forms, including personal crises, societal changes, and global events.

Strengthen your faith

Trust in God's guidance and presence in your life. Believe that He will give you the strength to overcome any challenge.

Make regular time for prayer and meditation to strengthen your connection with God and prepare yourself for the challenges ahead.

Community and Support

Build a strong network of faithful friends and church members who can support you in difficult times.

Use the resources of your church, such as Bible study groups, counseling, and service projects, to strengthen and encourage one another.

Continue learning

Continue your religious education and study of the scriptures to develop a deep understanding and strong foundation for your faith.

Remain open to new insights and experiences that can enrich and deepen your faith.

Encouragement to continually deepen and actively live your faith

Conscious faith is not just a retreat in difficult times, but an active, daily practice. It is important to continually deepen your faith and integrate it into all areas of your life.

Active participation

Attend church services and community events regularly to strengthen your faith and live in community.

Get involved in social projects and missions to live out your faith through practical action.

Reflection and Spiritual Growth

Use times of reflection to reflect on your journey with God and identify areas of growth.
Set goals for your personal and spiritual development and work toward them on an ongoing basis.

Inspirational stories and quotes

Finally, we would like to share some inspirational stories and quotes that will encourage and motivate you to continue on the path of faith.

- Corrie ten Boom was a Dutch Christian woman who helped many Jews escape from the Nazis during World War II. Despite her imprisonment and the cruel conditions of the Ravensbrück concentration camp, she held on to her faith and spread hope and love among her fellow prisoners. After the war, she worked for reconciliation and healing.

Quote from Mother Teresa: "We cannot all do great things. But we can do small things with great love. This quote reminds us that every small act of love and faith can make a big difference.

- Dietrich Bonhoeffer, a German theologian and resistance fighter, remained true to his faith and fought against Nazi oppression. His courage and determination are a powerful testament to how faith can provide support and inspiration in the darkest of times.

Quote from Pope John Paul II: "Do not be afraid! Open, yes, open wide the doors for Christ!" This quote encourages us to courageously live our faith and let Christ into our lives, regardless of the challenges we face.

Conclusion

These inspiring stories and quotes should encourage and motivate you to continue on the path of faith. Every challenge you face is an opportunity to deepen your faith and show how strong and fulfilling a life of faith can be.

7.4 Concluding Remarks

Dear readers, with this final chapter, we would like to express our sincere gratitude to you. Your commitment to reading this book and engaging with the ideas it contains is a valuable step on your personal faith journey. We hope that the thoughts, stories, and guidance presented here have opened new perspectives and supported you on your journey.

Our special thanks go to all those who contributed to the creation of this book. Thank you to the many people who shared their inspiring stories and experiences with us. Your courage and willingness to speak openly about your faith journey made this book possible. Thank you to everyone who has supported and encouraged us in this project.

As we close this book, we would like to leave you with one last encouraging thought:

Conscious faith is a source of inexhaustible strength and profound joy. In a world often marked by uncertainty and change, faith in God offers a firm anchor and a source of peace. Let us encourage you to live and deepen this faith every day. Be open to the wonders that God can work in your life and remain steadfast in your relationship with Him.

May God bless you and accompany you in all your ways. May your faith always grow and strengthen and guide you in all situations of life. We wish you all the best in your journey of faith.

Appendix

The Story of Rosalind Wright Picard

Rosalind Wright Picard has been public about her conversion to Christianity since the early 2000s. Her first significant mention of her religious journey was in an interview published in 2010. Since then, she has shared her story in various forums and interviews, including a blog post in 2019 and an in-depth interview in 2021.

In her stories, she describes how she gradually transitioned from an atheist to a devout Christian through meeting educated Christians and reading the Bible. In particular, the influence of the wisdom she found in the Bible and the positive changes in her life after accepting the faith played a major role in her conversion.

Picard emphasizes that her faith has had a significant impact on her life and work without compromising her scientific integrity. She emphasizes that science and faith can coexist and that there are many ways to gain knowledge beyond the purely scientific method.

Rosalind Wright Picard is a remarkable electrical engineer and professor at MIT. Originally an atheist, she describes her conversion to faith as a multi-step process shaped by both her scientific career and her personal reflections.

Science and Faith

Picard emphasizes that many scientists too often assume that there is nothing that cannot be measured. She criticizes this attitude of "scientism" and argues that there are many ways to gain knowledge beyond the scientific method. These include historical evidence, personal experience, and the wisdom contained in religious texts such as the Bible.

She makes it clear that she values science and uses rigorous scientific methods in her work. However, it recognizes that science cannot capture all truths. The search for truth, which she says is at the heart of science, also requires a belief that there is truth to be discovered.

Her journey to Christianity

Picard describes how she used to see religion, and Christianity in particular, as a crutch for people who didn't understand science. But through meeting smart and educated believers and reading the Bible, her perspective changed. She began to explore Christianity and other religions more deeply, visiting various religious sites and realizing that many of her preconceptions were unfounded.

She was particularly influenced by the historical and intellectual aspects of Christianity. Gradually, she changed from an atheist to an agnostic to a theist and finally to a devout Christian. This change was not easy, but by practicing her faith, she experienced significant positive changes in her life.

Personal impact

Picard describes how faith in Jesus Christ has profoundly improved her life, giving her peace, joy, and wisdom. She emphasizes that Christianity is a gift for all people, regardless of their background or religion. This gift has not only enriched her life spiritually, but has also inspired her scientific work, as she is now even more in awe of what science can reveal.

Finally, she emphasizes that the relationship with God, like human relationships, grows through trust and action. Only through the active life of faith can one experience the deeper reality and truth.

The Conversion of Ayaan Hirsi Ali: A Plea for Faith

Ayaan Hirsi Ali, a prominent former atheist and advocate for enlightenment, has undergone a remarkable transformation. Originally known for her harsh criticism of Islam and her unwavering belief in reason and the secular values of the Enlightenment, Hirsi Ali now embraces Christianity and Christian values. In her latest interview, she talks about the profound challenges facing Western civilization and emphasizes the need to return to Christian roots and faith in God.

In her interview, Hirsi Ali highlights three main threats that are destroying Western civilization from within:

Forgetting one's roots: Hirsi Ali describes how Western society has neglected its historical and cultural roots, resulting in a collective amnesia. This forgetting leads to an identity crisis and makes society vulnerable to ideological attacks from within and without.

Romantic glorification and bad ideas: It criticizes the romantic glorification of past eras and the spread of destructive ideas such as neo-Marxism and identity politics. These ideas undermine the foundations of Western civilization and promote a culture of victimhood and division.

Education and critical thinking: Hirsi Ali emphasizes that modern education systems often promote ideological dogma rather than critical thinking and reflection. This has far-reaching consequences for society's ability to deal with the challenges of the present.

A call for a return to faith

Hirsi Ali argues passionately that faith in God and a return to Christian values are crucial to overcoming these challenges. She describes how faith not only brings spiritual fulfillment, but is also a source of strength and courage. In times of crisis, deep-rooted convictions and courage are needed to stand firm.

In keeping with the content of this book, Hirsi Ali emphasizes the importance of a conscious act of faith. Faith in God is not only a personal choice, but also an act of resistance against the forces that seek to destroy Western civilization. She calls us to actively live our faith, to defend Christian values, and to resist cultural amnesia.

An affirmation of our message

Ayaan Hirsi Ali's statements confirm and reinforce the central messages of this book. As we have argued throughout the chapters, the conscious decision to believe in God is a way to counter the loss of meaning and disorientation of modern society. Hirsi Ali's impressive change of heart and clear statements provide a powerful conclusion and encourage readers to apply the principles and practices discussed in the book to their own lives.

May this epilogue serve as an inspiring call to action, encouraging readers to deepen and actively live out their own faith. Together, let us defend the values and beliefs that have made our civilization strong and, through conscious faith in God, create a new foundation for a fulfilling and meaningful future.